M000280139

RICH MYERS

SENSATIONAL CAKES, BAKES & DESSERTS

GET BAKED ®

WHITE LION
PUBLISHING

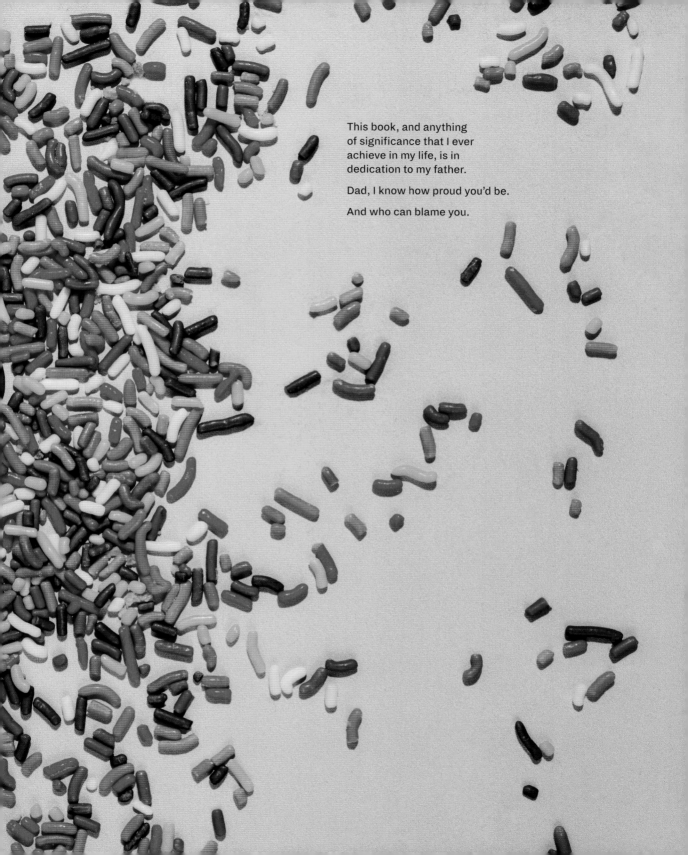

This book, and anything
of significance that I ever
achieve in my life, is in
dedication to my father.

Dad, I know how proud you'd be.

And who can blame you.

INTRODUCTION

I have been a lover of food for as long as I can remember. It's a passion that I inherited from my dad, and when I was a kid, I loved nothing more than spending my Saturdays watching countless hours of cookery shows with him.

I am not a trained chef, or pastry chef, or even a baker. It has always been my intention that GET BAKED® embodies a philosophy that spends less time focusing on complicated combinations and techniques that don't really matter and more time focusing on creating desserts that just taste delicious.

It might seem disingenuous to say this, considering this book contains a recipe for a preposterously large 24-layer chocolate cake, but I'm really not one for novelty. Every component of every recipe exists because it makes sense and elevates the finished product. There's a temptation in the bakery world nowadays to just shower everything with shop-bought chocolate bars and biscuits – you won't find any of that here.

I am known on social media as being someone that has somewhat of an unusual writing style – one that's particularly dry and, more often than not, a little bit out there. I have done everything I can, within the constraints of a recipe book, to impart as much of my personality as possible into the pages that follow.

Whether you're a die-hard GET BAKED® fan, or you've never heard of us and have just picked this up because you think it looks tasty, I hope you enjoy reading this book as much as I've enjoyed writing it.

That wasn't entirely honest because I haven't enjoyed writing it.

It's ruined my life for the last 9 months, but it's over now.

I don't mean my life's over, I mean the book's over because I've finished writing it.

My life has just begun, and so has yours.

KIT LIST

Note that all recipes were tested in a fan assisted oven.

Most of the stuff on this kit list is available from your favourite online retailers.

Before I carry on, you'll notice that the liquid measurements in this book are given in grams rather than millilitres. At GET BAKED®, we weigh everything, even water. This is more consistent and means you don't have to get down to eye level with a measuring jug every ten minutes of your life, which – let's be honest – nobody needs to be dealing with right now. So yeah, moral of the story, weigh your liquids. Weigh your eggs out of their shells (the average egg weighs approximately 50g/1¾oz if that helps).

Whenever you're doing anything that requires quite a few ingredients, it's always best to weigh everything out at the beginning, rather than weighing some stuff, preparing it, weighing more stuff, preparing it, and so on. Being organised makes everything a lot more fun, and weighing ingredients separately is amateur. In professional cookery, you'd refer to this as 'mise en place', which is French fancy talk for 'putting in place'. You're essentially a French patisserie chef now, so start acting like it.

You'll notice that all the sprinkles used in this book are my brand, expen$ive sprinkles. You could use any type of sprinkle in their place, but mine are superior.

→ Heatproof spatula (the bakery version of a spatula, not the thing you use to flip a burger)
→ Non-serrated cook's knife (make sure it's sharp because dull knives are a lot more dangerous than sharp ones)
→ Offset palette knife
→ Box grater
→ Pastry brush
→ Ice cream scoop (extremely useful for stuff like cookies and truffles)
→ Silicone baking mat
→ Cake turntable
→ Cake drum

→ Food-safe gloves
→ Blowtorch
→ Piping (pastry) bag
→ Candy thermometer/temperature probe
→ Cake-release spray
→ Cake scraper
→ Food processor
→ Stand mixer (attachments: balloon whisk, dough hook, beater)
→ 30cm (12in) fluted pie tin
→ 30 x 40cm (12 x 16in) rectangular cake tin
→ 23cm (9in) cake tins (7.5cm/3in deep)

CHOC
CHOC
CHOC

DARK CHOCOLATE TRUFFLES

MAKES
20 truffles

A classic chocolate truffle, made with only a handful of ingredients. Nothing says, 'Oh look at me and my nice kitchen' like pulling these out with some good-quality coffee when you're hosting a dinner party. What a load of nonsense that is though. I personally prefer making this sort of thing when I'm home alone. What's worse than inviting people to your house? Literally nothing.

Try steeping some Earl Grey tea bags in the cream overnight for a floral (and wholly unnecessary) middle-class addition to something that's already perfectly good as it is.

Also, there's no requirement to use cocoa powder to coat your truffles – it's just a classic way to finish them. You can use literally anything, within reason. Proceed with caution though: I once used French beans and it went down like a lead balloon.

INGREDIENTS

600g (1lb 5oz) 55–70% dark chocolate
600g (1lb 5oz) double (heavy) cream
5g (⅛oz) sea salt (Maldon is ideal)
approx. 50g (1¾oz) cocoa powder to coat (enough to fill a small bowl and cover the truffles)

METHOD

Make the ganache exactly the same way it's made in the recipe for Salted Dark Chocolate Ganache (see page 30).

Once emulsified, decant the ganache into a 5cm (2in)-deep tray and leave to cool at room temperature. Once the ganache has set, you're ready to make your truffles. You need to set up a little truffle station: place your cocoa powder (not French beans) into a small bowl, half-fill another small bowl with some warm water and place a teaspoon in the bowl of water to warm the spoon. You're also going to want a clean towel to dry off your spoon in between truffle scooping.

Using the teaspoon, scoop a truffle ball and drop it straight from the spoon into the bowl of cocoa powder. Carefully roll the truffle in the cocoa powder, then remove it from the bowl and place it on a clean tray lined with foil or greaseproof paper. Repeat the process until the mixture's all used up, remembering to dry your teaspoon in between scooping so that you don't end up with any excess water on your truffles.

Your truffles are good to eat straight away, but if you prefer a firmer bite, you can place them in the fridge, where they'll keep ever so happily for up to one month.

CAMPFIRE PIE

10 generous portions
or 14 normal portions

Campfire is one of those pies that'll always be on the menu at GET BAKED®. It's simple, looks impressive and tastes sensational. Its namesake takes inspiration from singing 'Kumbaya, my Lord' while toasting marshmallows at Cub Scouts as a youth. I never actually went to Cub Scouts and I've definitely never sung 'Kumbaya', but I feel like if I did, this pie would capture it exquisitely. If you've got friends coming over for drinks on a summer's evening, and you want to impress them, then it's Campfire, all day long.

INGREDIENTS

For the digestive biscuit crust

500g (1lb 2oz) chocolate
   digestive biscuits
5g (⅛oz) sea salt
200g (7oz) unsalted butter, cubed

For the filling

600g (1lb 5oz) Salted Dark
   Chocolate Ganache
   (see page 30)
500g (1lb 2oz) Italian meringue
   (see page 52)

To finish

10g (¼oz) 55–70% dark chocolate

METHOD

Blitz the chocolate digestive biscuits and salt to a fine crumb in a food processor, then decant into a mixing bowl. In a microwave-safe bowl, melt your butter for about 1 minute 30 seconds in the microwave, until it's totally melted. Add the melted butter to your bowl of crumbs and, using your hands, as they're the best tool for the job, thoroughly mix until it has the consistency of wet sand. It's important to make sure that there are no dry patches and that the butter is evenly distributed throughout the mixture. If the mix is feeling a little dry, melt another 50g (1¾oz) of butter and add a tablespoon at a time until you reach the desired consistency.

While it's still warm, transfer the mixture to a 30cm (12in) fluted pie dish and firmly press the crust into the pie dish using your knuckles, making sure to cover the sides as well as the base. There's no right or wrong way to do this, you're just pressing fun stuff into a pie dish. It can look as perfect or as rustic as you like, it really doesn't matter because ultimately the whole thing is going to be covered and you're hardly going to see any of it. Just enjoy yourself and stop taking everything so seriously – you're making a pie, not voting in a general election. Once your knuckles can't take any more, put the pie dish in the fridge to set. You can do this well in advance, even days before, which is great if you're hosting friends and want to actually enjoy yourself.

While your pie crust is chilling, make the Salted Dark Chocolate Ganache (see page 30). By the time you're done, the pie crust will be set. Pour the ganache into the pie crust and put it back in the fridge to set. It'll take at least 2 hours for your ganache to fully set, so during this time you can get on with your life and take comfort in the form of resting on a soft fabric.

→

When it comes to topping the pie with Italian meringue, you've got two options. You can pre-top the pie and put it back in the fridge, or you can top the pie right before serving, which looks impressive and will convince your guests that you're some sort of expert.

To top the pie, carefully spoon mounds of your pillowy-soft meringue on top of the ganache. It's important that you're not heavy-handed, because you'll knock too much air out of the meringue and it'll look less voluptuous. The idea is to create the appearance of flames: you can do this by flicking the meringue using the back of the spatula and pulling it up. Imagine the conductor of an orchestra flicking his wand-thing and re-enact the scene. You are the conductor, and the meringue is your orchestra.

When you're all flicked out, torch the meringue using a blowtorch. Don't hold the blowtorch over the same bit for too long, or you'll burn the meringue. The easiest way to ensure this doesn't happen is to place the pie on top of a cake turntable and turn the pie with one hand, while holding the blowtorch in the other. If you constantly turn the turntable, the meringue won't catch and you'll get a nice, even toasting.

To finish, using the finest side of a box grater, carefully grate the dark chocolate all over the top of your pie.

O.G. BROWNIES

MAKES

10–16 slices, depends how
big you want 'em

The original and the best. In my opinion brownies should NOT be cakey. Cakey consistencies are reserved for cakes. Brownies should be dense, fudgy and incredibly rich. Some 'bakers' try to fake it, by essentially serving underbaked brownies, and passing them off as 'gooey'. They're charlatans, and you shouldn't listen to them. If, after a few minutes in the oven, you notice a very thin, paper-like layer forming on top of your brownies, then congratulations, you've nailed it. If you don't, you've done something wrong along the way.

I'm not a charlatan. I'm just a young boy from West Yorkshire trying to help you on your path to baking delicious stuff.

INGREDIENTS

750g (1lb 10oz) caster (superfine)
  sugar
300g (10½oz) light brown sugar
520g (1lb 2½oz) 55% dark chocolate
520g (1lb 2½oz) unsalted butter,
  plus extra for greasing
460g (1lb ¼oz) eggs
380g (13½oz) plain (all-purpose)
  flour, sifted
140g (5oz) cocoa powder, sifted
5g (⅛oz) sea salt
icing (powdered) sugar,
  for dusting (optional)

METHOD

Preheat your oven to 160°C (320°F/gas 3).

Put the sugars in the bowl of a stand mixer fitted with the paddle attachment and set to one side while you melt the chocolate and butter together in a medium heavy-bottomed saucepan over a medium heat (if your chocolate is in bar form, chop the pieces first so that they melt more easily). You're going to need to stir often. If you don't stir it, and the chocolate catches at the bottom of the pan, your mixture is going to go grainy and the chocolate will taste bitter. There's really no way back from this, so don't let it happen.

While the mixture is melting, add your eggs to the sugars and mix on high speed for a few minutes, or until the mixture looks pale and airy. As soon as the mixture has reached this consistency, turn the mixer down to the lowest speed and wait for your chocolate mixture to finish emulsifying.

When the chocolate mixture looks glossy and there are no lumps, pour it directly into the sugar and eggs and continue to mix on low speed until everything has combined. At this point you'll need to scrape down the bottom and sides of the mixer bowl because there'll be some sugar stuck to it, and if you don't combine it at this stage, you'll get crunchy bits of sugar in your brownies, which isn't the worst thing to have ever happened in your life, but it's a pretty close second.

→ Remove the bowl from the stand mixer and add the flour, cocoa powder and salt. Fold them in using a spatula or wooden spoon, just until you can no longer see the dry ingredients. It's crucial that you don't overmix the flour, or you'll end up with a cakey brownie, which is my idea of hell on earth.

Shmear a 30 x 40cm (12 x 16in) rectangular cake tin with a generous helping of butter and line with baking parchment. It helps if you leave some excess baking parchment on two sides of the tin (roughly 5cm/2in above the edge of the tin) so you can pull the brownies out easily once they're cooked. Pour your brownie batter into the tin. Our recipe results in a particularly thick brownie batter, so you'll need to use a small offset palette knife or the back of a spoon to spread the mixture evenly across the tin.

Bake your brownie mixture in the oven for 25 minutes. It should still be gooey, and a toothpick inserted into the mixture should come out pretty filthy. If it comes out clean, you've overbaked and your brownies won't be as fudgy. They'll still be pretty good, but you've essentially failed.

Remove the tin from the oven and set it to one side until it's at room temperature – about 30 minutes should do it – then bang it into the fridge for at least 8 hours, ideally overnight. Setting in the fridge is absolutely crucial if you want to achieve the dense, fudgy brownie that we're known for. Once chilled, remove from the fridge and top with a generous helping of sifted icing (powdered) sugar. This is optional, but it's true to how we serve our O.G. Brownie.

Remove the slab from the tin and slice into brownies, as big or small as you want, I honestly don't care. They're pretty rich though, so you can slice smaller than you probably think is necessary. I recommend using a sharp, non-serrated cook's knife; you won't get a clean finish using a serrated knife. If you want to go all out, run the knife under the hot tap and then dry it off before slicing and clean the knife with warm water and a clean cloth in between each slice. Do this and your brownies will look utterly sensational.

Once sliced, they'll keep for up to 7 days in an airtight container, and it's up to you whether or not you keep them in the fridge. At GET BAKED®, we serve them cold, straight from the fridge, because I really like them that way, but it's your rodeo. They also freeze incredibly well, and will be good for up to a month.

H$_2$O TRUFFLES

MAKES
20 truffles

These are the purest form of chocolate truffle that one can make. They're amazing for so many reasons. They contain hardly any ingredients and they're ridiculously easy to make.

These truffles make use of a 'water ganache' which essentially replaces the cream in a regular ganache recipe with water. A lot of pastry chefs actually prefer a water ganache because it allows you to experience chocolate in its truest form, without the flavour and textural addition of cream. It is absolutely imperative that you use high-quality chocolate, because ultimately that's pretty much all you're going to taste.

INGREDIENTS

600g (1lb 5oz) 55–70% dark chocolate
600g (1lb 5oz) still water (tap is fine, we're not all made of money)
5g (⅛oz) sea salt (Maldon is ideal)
25g (1oz) chopped nuts of your choice

METHOD

Make your Salted Dark Chocolate Ganache (see page 30) but replace the cream with water. Treat the water exactly the same way the cream is treated in the recipe, ensuring that it doesn't come to a rolling boil. After you pour the water into the bowl of chocolate, the chocolate will seize and it'll look awful, because water is chocolate's worst enemy, but as you stir the mixture, they will be forced to emulsify, eventually becoming one. The ganache will look thinner than if you used cream, which is common sense really because water is thinner than cream.

Once emulsified, decant the ganache into a 5cm (2in)-deep tray and leave to cool at room temperature. Once the ganache has set, you're ready to make your truffles. You need to set up a little truffle station: place your chopped nuts into a small bowl, half-fill another small bowl with some warm water and place a teaspoon in the bowl of water to warm the spoon. You're also going to want a clean towel to dry off your spoon in between truffle scooping.

Using the teaspoon, scoop a truffle ball and drop it straight from the spoon into the bowl of chopped nuts. Carefully roll the truffle in the nuts, then remove it from the bowl and place it on a clean tray lined with foil or greaseproof paper. Repeat the process until you're all outta truffle, remembering to dry your teaspoon in between scooping so that you don't end up with any excess water on your truffles.

Your truffles are good to eat straight away, but if you prefer a firmer bite, you can place them in the fridge, where they'll keep ever so happily for up to one month.

TRIPLE CHOCOLATE BROWNIES

MAKES

10–16 slices, depends how big
you want 'em

INGREDIENTS

For the brownie

750g (1lb 10oz) caster
  (superfine) sugar
300g (10½oz) light brown sugar
520g (1lb 2½oz) 55% dark
  chocolate
520g (1lb 2½oz) unsalted butter,
  plus extra for greasing
380g (13½oz) plain (all-purpose)
  flour, sifted
460g (1lb ¼oz) eggs
140g (5oz) cocoa powder, sifted
5g (⅛oz) sea salt

For the triple chocolate topping

400g (14oz) Dark Chocolate
  Ganache (see page 30)
100g (3½oz) milk chocolate
  (chopped up if in bar form)
100g (3½oz) white chocolate
  (chopped up if in bar form)

The addition of ganache and lashings of melted chocolate takes our O.G. Brownie recipe to a whole new level. If you thought they were rich before, prepare to get loaded.

METHOD

Follow the recipe for the O.G. Brownies (see page 18).

Once your brownies have chilled, remove from the fridge and cut into slices. You're going to be topping the underside of your O.G. Brownies instead of the top. If the brownies are well made, the papery layer on top will mean that topping them is messy and unnecessarily difficult. That's why we top the underneath, where they're perfectly flat.

Your brownies will look much better if your ganache is a thin, glossy liquid, so ideally, it's best to make it now rather than use pre-made, but it's not the end of the world if you don't. It just means they'll look less professional, and it'll be more likely that the people eating them have even less respect for you than they do now. If you're using pre-made ganache, you're going to need to make sure you re-melt it in 10-second bursts in the microwave. Thoroughly stirring in between each burst is crucial, or the ganache will overheat in certain spots and probably split.

When you've got a thin and glossy dark chocolate ganache, dip your brownies into it one by one. Remember, you're topping the underneath of the brownies. You can submerge them as far as you desire into the warm chocolatey liquid. At GET BAKED®, we cover about a third of the brownie in ganache, but you can cover the whole damn thing if you want. Once topped, place them onto a greaseproof paper-lined baking tray, ensuring the brownies aren't touching, or they'll stick together as the ganache sets, which is just annoying.

While the ganache is setting, melt the milk and white chocolate, separately, not together, in short bursts of about 20 seconds in the microwave. Make sure you stir in between each burst, or it'll burn and you'll be wasting chocolate, which is a crime and a filthy one at that.

When your chocolates are melted, it's time to channel your inner Jackson Pollock. Use the back of a spoon to flick the chocolate all over the ganache-topped brownies, the more abstract, the better. They say baking is all about science, but this right here is an art, and the spoon is your paintbrush. Flick away. Your Triple Chocolate Brownies will keep for up to 3 days in a sealed container in the fridge.

S'MORES BROWNIES

MAKES

10–16 slices, depends how big
you want 'em

The textural marriage of dense, rich brownie and pillowy-soft meringue really is something to behold. When you throw into the mix the chewy, caramelised crust that you get when you set it on fire, the whole thing just gets downright ridiculous.

Making the meringue well can take a bit of practice, but it's a bit like riding a bike, without the whole braking too suddenly and flying face-first over the handlebars while Danny Griffin laughs about how much of a loser you are. It's not like that. I'm over it anyway.

INGREDIENTS

For the brownie

750g (1lb 10oz) caster
  (superfine) sugar
300g (10½oz) light brown sugar
520g (1lb 2½oz) 55% dark chocolate
520g (1lb 2½oz) unsalted butter,
  plus extra for greasing
460g (1lb ¼oz) eggs
380g (13½oz) plain (all-purpose)
  flour, sifted
140g (5oz) cocoa powder, sifted
5g (⅛oz) sea salt

For the Italian meringue topping

240g (8½oz) caster
  (superfine) sugar
80g (2¾oz) cold water
130g (4½oz) egg whites
½ tsp vanilla extract
a few digestive biscuits, crushed,
  to finish

METHOD

Follow the recipe for the O.G. Brownies (see page 18).

Once your brownies have chilled, remove from the fridge and slice your brownies into 10–16 slices using a sharp cook's knife.

Follow the instructions on page 52 to make your Italian meringue. You're probably going to make it wrong, and it won't be as good as it would have been if I'd made it for you, but there's really nothing anyone can do about that. If by some miracle you've pulled it off, transfer the meringue into a piping (pastry) bag.

I don't use any fancy nozzles because I can't be bothered, and I just don't see the point. You get just as nice a finish without using one, but if you really must, then go ahead and make it look all pretty. Pipe your meringue onto the underside of your brownies (which should be perfectly flat) in whatever style makes you feel good about yourself. I personally like to go for the straight lines on an angle look, because it shows people that I'm capable of precision, but that I also still have a bit of personality left in me. Just a quick one: if you go for a big blob in the middle, everyone will know you're a loser, so don't do that. The same can be said for any sort of flower pattern, although that's actually even worse.

When you're all piped out, toast the meringue using a blowtorch and finish off the whole ordeal with some digestive biscuit crumbs.

These brownies are best eaten on the day you make them, but if that ain't gonna work, you can store the O.G. Brownies in a sealed container for up to 7 days and then top with the Italian meringue before serving.

SALTED CHOCOLATE COOKIES

MAKES

10 cookies

Our cookies are quite thin: they're a classic crispy on the edges, chewy on the outside and soft in the middle type of affair. If you're looking for anything else, you've come to the wrong place.

INGREDIENTS

140g (5oz) softened unsalted butter
110g (3¾oz) caster (superfine) sugar
140g (5oz) light brown sugar
1 tsp vanilla extract
1 egg
140g (5oz) plain (all-purpose) flour, sifted
140g (5oz) strong white bread flour, sifted
1 tsp baking powder
1 tsp bicarbonate of soda (baking soda)
1 tsp sea salt, plus an extra pinch to finish
250g (9oz) 55% dark chocolate buttons, or a bar chopped into chunks

METHOD

Start by creaming the butter and sugars together in the bowl of a stand mixer fitted with the beater attachment until pale and fluffy. Add the vanilla to your egg, then add to the butter and sugar mixture. Using the beater attachment, mix for 1 minute, or until emulsified, then scrape down the base and sides of the bowl. Weigh out the flours, baking powder, bicarbonate of soda (baking soda) and salt and add to the bowl. Beat on the lowest speed until the mixture comes together. Add the chocolate and beat until it's mixed evenly throughout.

Using an ice cream scoop, or your hands, scoop the mixture into ten 100g (3½oz) pucks and place onto a greaseproof paper-lined tray. Cover the tray in cling film (plastic wrap) and put it into the fridge for at least 24 hours (at most 72 hours). Letting the pucks chill before baking them makes all the difference. It gives the cookies a depth of flavour that you just can't achieve without letting them rest. Be patient – your cookies will be good if you rush the process, but sensational if you don't. If you absolutely must bake the cookies on the same day, try to give them at least 6 hours to chill before baking.

When you're ready to bake, preheat your oven to 150°C (300°F/gas 2). Split the ten pucks across two greaseproof paper-lined baking trays, leaving enough space between them to allow for spreading in the oven.

Bake for 12–15 minutes, or until the cookies resemble cookies. If they're still bulging in the centre, then they're not ready yet. Remove from the oven and sprinkle with sea salt while still warm (if you wait until they've cooled, the salt won't stick). The salt really helps to bring out the flavour of the chocolate, but don't use too much, or it'll taste salty, and quite literally nobody wants a salty cookie.

The cookies will keep for up to 2 days in an airtight container but are best eaten on the day you make them. Don't be tempted to eat them when they're still hot out of the oven, because despite what you see in the movies, they need time to rest, and a cookie fresh out of the oven is nowhere near as good as you'd hope it would be.

SALTED DARK CHOCOLATE GANACHE

MAKES

Approx. 600g (1lb 5oz), or enough to top a Campfire Pie (see page 14)

Ganache is a staple in any baker's kitchen. There's nothing complicated going on here, it's just an emulsification of chocolate and cream, but in the wrong hands it'll turn into an oily, grainy mess. What you're about to read should ensure that doesn't happen. I'll also tell you how to fix it when stuff goes wrong.

INGREDIENTS

300g (10½oz) 55–70% good-quality dark chocolate (the better the chocolate, the better the ganache)
300g (10½oz) double (heavy) cream
5g (⅛oz) sea salt (Maldon ideally, it's just better that way)

METHOD

Okay let's start with the chocolate. If it's in bar form, you're going to need to chop it using a non-serrated cook's knife. The finer you chop the chocolate, the easier it'll melt with the cream, but small chunks are totally fine. If you're using buttons (or callets as we call them in the industry) or chocolate chips then you're good to go. Put your chocolate into a stainless steel or heatproof glass bowl and set aside.

Heat your cream in a small, heavy-bottomed saucepan over a medium heat. Use a heatproof silicone spatula to gently stir the cream so that it doesn't catch at the bottom of the pan. If your cream scalds, you'll see burnt bits in the pan. At this point it's Goodnight Vienna and you'll be starting again, so it's important that you don't leave the cream to its own devices. Don't get impatient and be tempted to turn up the heat, just relax and enjoy stirring the cream. You don't want to boil the cream, you want to take it to a simmer. When you see small bubbles forming and the cream has been steaming for a few seconds, remove from the heat and pour it directly onto your chocolate.

Don't even think about touching the chocolate and cream for a few minutes. If you start stirring straight away, you're going to cool the cream down too soon, so just let the hot cream do its thing and melt the chocolate itself for a while. After two minutes, using the same heatproof spatula, stir the chocolate and cream until the mixture is glossy and smooth and the chocolate has totally melted. The best advice anyone ever gave me when it comes to mixing ingredients in a bowl is to look after the sides, and the middle will look after itself.

So, at this point, one of three things will have happened:

1. You have a silky-smooth mixture that resembles the best chocolate sauce you've ever seen in your life.

2. You have a nice mixture, but there's some chocolate still in there that just won't melt.

3. You have split the ganache, and it looks bad. Very bad.

GET BAKED

If you've got some chocolate in there that hasn't melted, just fill a saucepan a third full of water and put it over a medium heat. When the water begins to boil, turn the heat all the way down and place your bowl over the water. Congratulations, you have mastered the bain-marie. Using your spatula, mix the ganache until the chocolate has melted and then remove the bowl from the heat immediately. If you overheat the ganache, you will split the mixture.

If you've split the ganache, it's not the end of the world, it's just another few minutes of your life that you'll never get back. The easiest way to bring back a split ganache is by adding cold water to your mixture one teaspoon at a time until your ganache emulsifies and looks glossy. Once your ganache looks sensational, add the salt. The salt brings out the natural flavour of the chocolate and just makes it more chocolatey. It won't make your ganache salty, just make sure you use the measurements I've suggested.

At this point, your ganache is ready, however there's one more step you can take to ensure that it's perfectly smooth, and to be honest, it will make all the difference. Even though your ganache might look silky, there's probably tiny bits of chocolate that haven't totally melted. If you have a stick blender, I would strongly recommend giving the mixture some more of your time and blending it for around 5 minutes, ensuring that you keep the blender submerged at all times or you'll incorporate air into the ganache. Like I said, this isn't essential and your ganache will be fine if you don't do this, but if you do it'll be exceptional.

You can use your ganache straight away as a glaze for chocolate cake, or pour it into a pie crust for one of the layers in one of our pie recipes. Alternatively, you can directly cover the surface of the mixture with cling film (plastic wrap) – so that it doesn't form a skin – and keep it refrigerated for up to a month. As your ganache cools, it'll set and become spreadable. After a few hours at room temperature, it'll be the perfect consistency to use for a layer cake, either in between the sponge layers or around the outside.

TIP To make Boozy Ganache, swap out half of the double (heavy) cream for 150g (5½oz) of your favourite alcoholic spirit. I really love using a good-quality bourbon – it works so well with chocolate. Another great shout is vodka. It's not my drink of choice whatsoever, but it's actually a great pairing with good-quality dark chocolate.

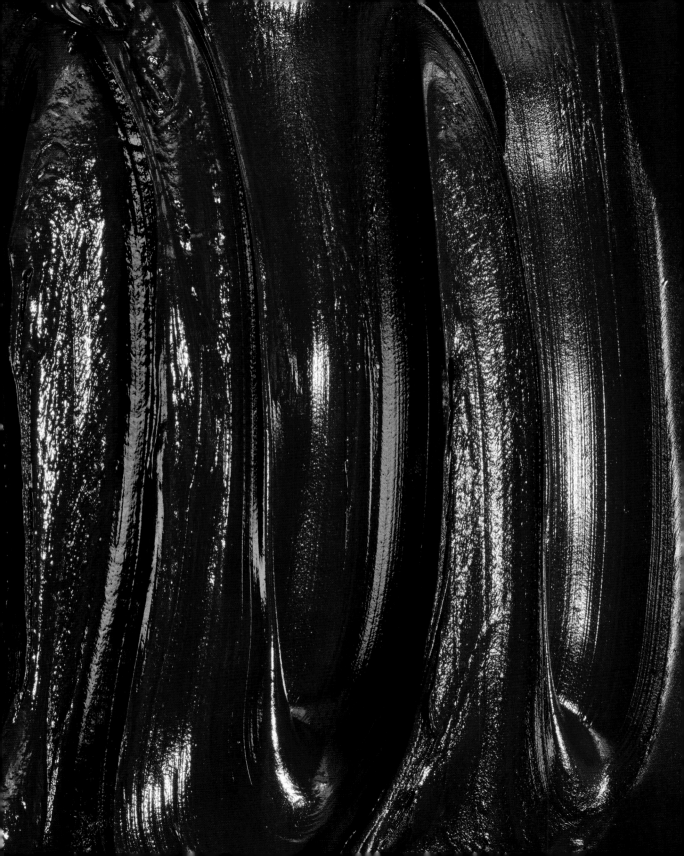

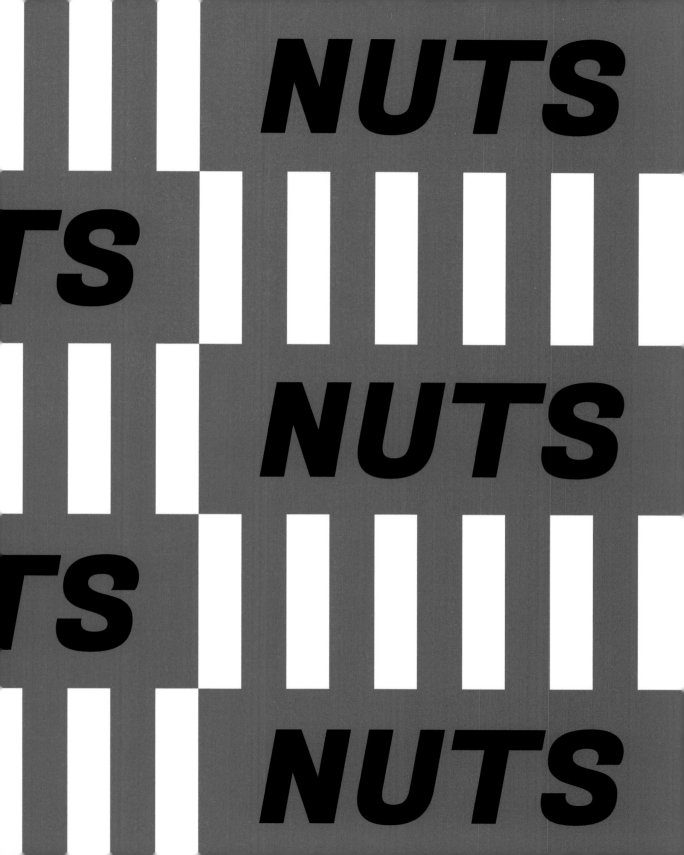

PBJ PIE

SERVES
10–14

It's the classic American combo, but in pie form. Steer clear of the new-age peanut butters that are better for your health. You're going to need proper old school peanut butter.

INGREDIENTS

For the digestive biscuit crust
700g (1lb 9oz) digestive biscuits
5g (⅛oz) sea salt
350g (12oz) unsalted butter, cubed
250g (9oz) raspberry jam

For the peanut butter ganache
500g (1lb 2oz) white chocolate
300g (10½oz) smooth peanut butter
300g (10½oz) double (heavy) cream

For the raspberry cream
50g (1¾oz) freeze-dried raspberries
500g (1lb 2oz) double (heavy) cream
Pink food colouring
   (use as suggested on packaging)

METHOD

Blitz the digestive biscuits and salt in a food processor (or with a rolling pin) to a fine crumb, then decant into a mixing bowl. Melt your butter in the microwave in a microwave-safe container for about 1 minute and 30 seconds, or until it's totally melted. Add the melted butter to your bowl of crumbs and mix thoroughly, making sure there are no dry patches. Press the mixture into your 30cm (12in) pie tin while the mixture is still warm. If you leave it too long, it'll become much less pliable. You can make your pie crust in advance and freeze it for up to a month – it won't lose any quality whatsoever.

Once you've lined your tin, bang it in the fridge for 10 minutes to firm up. After 10 minutes, evenly spread the raspberry jam onto the crust and put it back in the fridge.

Now onto the peanut butter ganache. Heat the double (heavy) cream, white chocolate and peanut butter in a heavy-bottomed saucepan over a very low heat. White chocolate splits notoriously easily, so be very careful not to overheat the mixture. Stir thoroughly using a heatproof spatula, paying extra attention to the bottom and sides of the pan. Take the ganache off the heat when you can still see a small amount of white chocolate pieces. If you continue to stir, the heat inside the pan will melt the remaining chocolate.

When the ganache is smooth, pour it on top of the raspberry jam and put it into the fridge to chill. While your ganache is chilling, get on with making your raspberry cream. To do this, first blitz your freeze-dried raspberries in a food processor, or using a pestle and mortar. You want them to resemble a very fine sand. Then put the double cream, pink food colouring and most of the raspberry dust into the bowl of a stand mixer fitted with the whisk attachment and whisk using the method for Properly Whipped Cream on page 84. Once whipped, put it into a piping (pastry) bag and pipe large blobs all over the top of the set peanut butter ganache layer. You don't need to pipe it on, you could just spread it using the back of a spoon, but sometimes it's nice to put a bit of effort in.

Finish by sprinkling some more raspberry dust over the top. PBJ will keep perfectly well for up to 3 days in the fridge.

PEANUT BRITTLE

MAKES

Enough to make your
mother-in-law realise that
you're better than she is

You can replace the peanuts in this recipe for any other nut that you might prefer if peanuts aren't your thing. You're going to need a silicone baking mat, although baking parchment will suffice, but a silicone mat is inexpensive and you'll get plenty of use out of it.

INGREDIENTS

100g (3½oz) flaked shelled
  peanuts (blanched and unsalted)
475g (1lb ½oz) caster
  (superfine) sugar
160g (5½oz) cold water

METHOD

Toast your peanuts in a dry frying pan (skillet) over a medium heat for around 3–4 minutes, tossing them every minute or so to make sure that they don't catch and burn. Toasting the peanuts is essential, because it'll release the oils and bring out all of the nutty flavour that you expect to get from a peanut. If you miss this step, you'll hardly taste them in your brittle. When the air is filled with a nutty aroma and your peanuts have started to take on a light brown colour, turn off the heat and leave them to rest in the pan.

Combine the caster (superfine) sugar and water in a heavy-bottomed saucepan, give it a stir to ensure that there's no sugar stuck to the bottom of the pan, and place over a medium heat. You're making what's called a 'wet caramel', because it's got water in it. A 'dry caramel' would just be sugar, but a wet caramel works best for this recipe as it is slightly thinner. Don't leave the pan unattended, because caramel has an incredibly annoying habit of burning when you leave it to its own devices, but don't mess around with it either.

It's handy to have a small bowl of water and a pastry brush to hand to brush some water down the sides of the pan, as any exposed sugar around the edge of the pan may start to crystallise. You'll notice the colour of the sugar syrup starting to turn golden. At first, it'll just be the teeniest glimmer of amber, but as it continues to reduce, you'll see the colour changing quite quickly. When your caramel reaches a deep amber colour, remove the pan from the heat and carefully add the toasted peanuts. Using a heatproof silicone spatula, mix the peanuts into the caramel and then pour it into the middle of a baking sheet lined with a silicone mat. You can use the spatula to help the caramel disperse itself evenly across the mat.

Set to one side and leave to cool for 30 minutes. The caramel will be incredibly hot, so be careful when lifting the baking sheet. When you come back to the caramel, it should have turned to brittle and be see-through, like a stained-glass window. A nut ridden, caramel-laden stained-glass window.

PEANUT AND CARAMEL BROWNIES

MAKES

10–16 slices, depends how
big you want 'em

I know what you're thinking. They look messy don't they. They are messy. They're very messy. There's nothing wrong with a bit of mess every now and again. Out of chaos comes clarity (I just made that up).

INGREDIENTS

For the brownie

750g (1lb 10oz) caster
  (superfine) sugar
300g (10½oz) light brown sugar
520g (1lb 2½oz) 55% dark chocolate
520g (1lb 2½oz) unsalted butter,
  plus extra for greasing
460g (1lb ¼oz) eggs
380g (13½oz) plain (all-purpose)
  flour, sifted
140g (5oz) cocoa powder, sifted
5g (⅛oz) sea salt

For the peanut butter and dark chocolate ganache

500g (1lb 2oz) 55% dark chocolate
  (chopped up if in bar form)
50g (1¾oz) smooth peanut butter
500g (1lb 2oz) double (heavy) cream

To finish

500g (1lb 2oz) Caramel
  (see page 102)
100g (3½oz) unsalted
  flaked peanuts

METHOD

Follow the recipe for the O.G. Brownies (see page 18).

To make the ganache, put the dark chocolate and peanut butter in a mixing bowl and pour the double (heavy) cream into a heavy-bottomed saucepan. Warm the cream over a medium heat until it comes to a simmer then immediately pour it on top of the chocolate and peanut butter. Leave for a minute or two, then use a heatproof spatula to mix the ingredients until combined. For tips on making ganache, see the Salted Dark Chocolate Ganache recipe (page 30).

When you've got a glossy ganache, dip your brownies into it one by one, remembering to top the underneath of the brownies, not the papery top. Once topped, place them onto a greaseproof paper-lined baking tray, ensuring the brownies aren't touching.

While the ganache sets, follow the recipe on page 102 to make the caramel. While the caramel is cooling, toast the peanuts in a dry frying pan over a medium heat for a few minutes, tossing occasionally. You'll know the peanuts are ready because they'll release their oils, and you'll get a strong whiff of peanuts. They'll also start to darken slightly. Make sure you don't burn them, or they'll taste bitter. Once toasted, leave to cool.

By now, your ganache will be set. If your caramel is still too warm, and hasn't thickened up enough yet to be pipeable, you can bang it in the fridge for ten minutes to speed up the process. The consistency that you're looking for is somewhere in between spoonable and pourable. If that makes sense, that's what you're looking for. If it doesn't, then I can't help you.

Spoon or pour (or sort of pour while spooning at the same time) the caramel into a piping (pastry) bag. Pipe lines of caramel onto the ganache and immediately top with the toasted peanuts.

Leave to set at room temperature until your caramel cools and thickens. Store the brownies in an airtight container for up to 3 days, or in the fridge for up to 5 days. They'll freeze incredibly well, even with the toppings on, for up to one month.

MR PISTACHIO PIE

SERVES

10–14

I love pistachio. Like, I really love pistachio. It all started in Venice's Lido di Jesolo in 1993. I was five years old, and we got some gelato. I didn't even know what pistachio was, I just remember thinking 'this green ice cream is sensational'.

Nobody other than my wife knows this, but a few years ago I had an Instagram account called 'Monsieur Pistache' where I reviewed pistachio ice cream from around the world. I say from around the world, but it only actually stretched as far as Blackpool. Either way, it was a thoroughly enjoyable couple of weeks. I gave up because no one cared enough to follow me.

INGREDIENTS

For the toasted waffle crust

250g (9oz) shop-bought
  Belgian waffles
250g (9oz) oat biscuits
5g (⅛oz) sea salt
300g (10½oz) unsalted butter, cubed

For the pistachio ganache

300g (10½oz) double (heavy) cream
500g (1lb 2oz) white chocolate
  (chopped up if in bar form)
300g (10½oz) pistachio crème

For the raspberry mallow

50g (1¾oz) freeze-dried
  raspberries, plus extra to decorate
500g (1lb 2oz) Italian meringue
  (see page 52)

METHOD

Preheat your oven to 180°C (350°F/gas 4).

Blitz the Belgian waffles to a fine crumb in a food processor (or bash the hell out of them with a rolling pin). Once you've pulverised the living daylights out of them, bang the crumbs on a baking tray and toast in your oven for 15 minutes or until they've browned slightly and your kitchen smells utterly sensational. While your waffles are in the oven, pulverise the oat biscuits and decant them into a mixing bowl. Add your toasted waffle crumb and sea salt to the bowl and give everything a mix.

Melt your butter in the microwave in a heatproof, microwave-safe container until it's totally melted. About 1 minute 30 seconds should do it. Add the melted butter to your bowl of crumbs and mix thoroughly using your hands, ensuring even distribution of melted butter. You don't want any dry patches, not now, not ever.

Press the mixture into your 30cm (12in) pie tin straight away, while the mixture is still warm, making sure to line the sides as well as the base. If you leave it too long, the butter will set, and it'll become much less pliable. If you like, you can make this in advance, and then just reheat the crumb in the microwave in short 15-second blasts.

Once you've lined your tin, bang it in the fridge to firm up for 10 minutes. If you're that way inclined, you can make your pie crusts in advance and freeze them. They'll be good in the freezer for up to a month and won't lose any quality whatsoever.

Now onto the pistachio ganache. Put the double (heavy) cream, white chocolate and pistachio crème in a heavy-bottomed saucepan and place over a very low heat, stirring continuously with a heatproof spatula. Be very careful not to overheat the mixture, because white chocolate splits notoriously easily. I'd recommend removing it from the heat every 30 seconds or so, so that it doesn't get too hot. As you stir, pay extra-close attention to the bottom and sides of the pan. Remove the pan from the heat when you can still see a small amount of white chocolate pieces. If you continue to stir, the heat still inside the pan will melt the remaining chocolate without it getting too hot.

When the ganache is smooth, pour it into the toasted waffle crust and put it into the fridge to chill. While your ganache is chilling, get on with making your raspberry mallow. To do this, first blitz your freeze-dried raspberries in a food processor, or a pestle and mortar. You want them to resemble a very fine sand, which isn't difficult, because they break apart like nobody's business. Our raspberry mallow is actually just Italian meringue with raspberry in it. I just like the word mallow. Sue me. Anyway, to make the fraudulent mallow, follow the Italian meringue recipe on page 52. When the meringue is just about ready, pour in the raspberry dust and continue to whisk until the meringue turns pink and tastes all fruity.

When the meringue/mallow/lies and deceit is ready, dollop mounds of it all over your freshly chilled pistachio pie. Once the bowl is empty, and the pie is covered, place it on a cake turntable and, using a small offset palette knife, smooth out the mallow (lies) while turning the pie. It's very hard to explain this in words, and I'm close to giving up. Look at the photo and try to copy that. If it doesn't work, it doesn't really matter because it will still taste good. Finish the pie by blitzing another small handful of freeze-dried raspberries and sprinkling them on top.

To enjoy him at his absolute best, serve Mr Pistachio on the day he's made. He can be kept in the fridge overnight, but his raspberry cape of lies will start to lose its voluptuousness and I genuinely can't believe that's a word.

SMOKY PECAN COOKIES

MAKES
10 cookies

The smoked sea salt in this recipe changes the whole dynamic of the situation entirely. If you've never tried it, you're missing out. The savoury notes that you get from the smoky salt make for a truly unique cookie experience.

INGREDIENTS

For the cookies

140g (5oz) softened unsalted butter
110g (3¾oz) caster (superfine) sugar
140g (5oz) light brown sugar
1 tsp vanilla extract
1 egg
140g (5oz) plain (all-purpose) flour, sifted
140g (5oz) strong white bread flour, sifted
1 tsp baking powder
1 tsp bicarbonate of soda (baking soda)
1 tsp sea salt
100g (3½oz) pecan halves, roughly chopped

To finish

150g (5½oz) Caramel (see page 102)
1 tsp smoked sea salt, for the top (Maldon make a great smoked sea salt)

METHOD

Start by creaming the butter and sugars together in the bowl of a stand mixer fitted with the beater attachment until pale and fluffy. Add the vanilla to your egg, then add to the butter and sugar mixture. Using the beater attachment, mix for 1 minute, or until emulsified, then scrape down the base and sides of the bowl. Weigh out the flours, baking powder, bicarbonate of soda (baking soda) and salt, and add to the bowl. Beat on the lowest speed until the mixture comes together. Add the chopped pecans and beat until it's mixed evenly throughout.

Using an ice cream scoop, or your hands, scoop the mixture into ten 100g (3½oz) pucks and place onto a greaseproof paper-lined tray. Cover the tray in clingfilm (plastic wrap) and put it into the fridge for at least 24 hours (at most 72 hours). If you absolutely must bake the cookies on the same day, try to give them at least 6 hours to chill before baking.

When you're ready to bake, preheat your oven to 150°C (300°F/gas 2). Split the ten pucks across two greaseproof paper-lined baking trays, leaving enough space between them to allow for spreading in the oven. Our cookies are quite thin: they're a classic, crispy on the edges, chewy on the outside, and soft in the middle type of affair.

Bake for 12–15 minutes, or until the cookies resemble cookies. If they're still bulging in the centre, then they're not ready yet. When they're baked, leave to cool. While they're resting, make the caramel using the recipe on page 102. By the time you've finished making your caramel, your cookies will be cool enough to finish. Finish them by throwing caramel all over them in the most aggressive fashion you can muster. Move your shoulders and everything. The application of the caramel onto the cookies requires a full body workout. You should be dripping with sweat post caramelisation. Then, when you can hardly move, sprinkle the smoked sea salt on top.

The cookies will keep for up to 2 days in an airtight container but are best eaten on the day you make them. Don't be tempted to eat them when they're still hot out of the oven; they need time to rest.

PIETRO PIE

SERVES

10–14

I named this pie after the fella that founded Ferrero. Can you imagine being the man responsible for introducing Nutella to the world? I can't even begin to think how much this guy must have loved hazelnuts. There's a rumour going round that he would only bathe in water filtered through his beloved nuts. But it's not true – I made it up.

INGREDIENTS

For the chocolate biscuit crust

500g (1lb 2oz) bourbon biscuits
5g (⅛oz) sea salt
200g (7oz) unsalted butter, cubed

For the chocolate cremeux

125g (4¼oz) 55% dark chocolate, chopped up if in bar form
100g (3½oz) whole milk
100g (3½oz) double (heavy) cream
30g (1oz) egg yolk
30g (1oz) caster (superfine) sugar

For the hazelnut ganache

250g (9oz) 70% dark chocolate, chopped up if in bar form
250g (9oz) double (heavy) cream
5g (⅛oz) sea salt
250g (9oz) Nutella
500g (1lb 2oz) hazelnut crème

To finish

50g (1¾oz) roasted hazelnuts, chopped

METHOD

Blitz the bourbon biscuits and salt in a food processor to a fine crumb (or use a rolling pin), then decant into a mixing bowl. Melt your butter in the microwave in a microwave-safe container until it's totally melted. About 1 minute 30 seconds should do it. Add the melted butter to your bowl of crumbs and mix thoroughly, ensuring even distribution of melted butter. Press the mixture into your 30cm (12in) pie tin straight away. If you like, you can make this in advance, and then just reheat the crumb in the microwave in short 15-second blasts.

Once you've lined your tin, bang it in the fridge to firm up. Ten minutes later it's ready to fill. You can make your pie crust in advance and freeze it for up to a month – it won't lose any quality whatsoever.

Now, make the chocolate cremeux. Cremeux is a fancy name for a thick chocolate custard. It's sensational, and once you've nailed it, you'll want to put it on everything. Including your partner.

First, melt the dark chocolate in short, 30 second bursts in the microwave and set to one side. Mix the milk and cream together in a heavy-bottomed saucepan and gently warm over a low heat. Meanwhile, use a small balloon whisk to whisk the egg yolk and sugar together in a bowl until pale – a minute or so should do it. When the milk and cream mixture is hot, but not boiling, pour a small amount over the eggs and sugar and whisk to combine. This is to temper the eggs, to ensure that they don't scramble. If you added them straight to the hot cream, they could cook, and your custard would be lumpy. This most likely wouldn't actually happen, but it's better to be safe than sorry.

Once combined, pour the eggs, sugar and cream mixture into the pan and stir. Do not stop stirring. The mixture will now start to thicken and resemble custard. Use a probe thermometer to monitor the temperature, because you don't want it to get above 82°C (180°F). It's best to keep the heat low, so you have more control over what's going on – if it's too hot, it'll start to boil and things will get a bit stressful.

→ Just take your time, you're making custard not representing your country in the Olympics. As soon as the temperature has reached 82°C (180°F), remove from the heat and pour straight onto your melted chocolate.

Leave for 1 minute before stirring, so you don't knock all of the heat out of the bowl. After a minute, stir the custard into the chocolate until smooth. Try a bit on your finger at this point – it'll be a proper dreamy mixture and quite honestly you won't believe it's you that actually made it. Once the cremeux is smooth, cover the mixture directly with cling film (plastic wrap) so that it doesn't form a skin and leave to cool at room temperature.

Make the hazelnut ganache by combining the dark chocolate, double (heavy) cream, salt and Nutella in a saucepan. Stir continually over a very low heat. Remove the pan from the heat every minute or so, continuing to stir, to lower the temperature. Put back on the heat and repeat until the ganache is glossy. Pour directly into the biscuit crust and place back in the fridge to set. After about half an hour, add the layer of hazelnut crème. You can buy hazelnut crème from supermarkets and online retailers (try searching for 'white chocolate hazelnut spread'). Melt the crème in a bowl in the microwave (or in a heavy-bottomed saucepan over a medium heat) until thin and runny. Pour on top of the hazelnut ganache layer and use the back of a spoon to evenly spread.

By now, the cremeux should have cooled enough to be put in the fridge. It thickens as it cools and it'll need at least a few hours in the fridge before it's ready to use. You might want to make it a day in advance so that you're not spending your life waiting for custard to thicken – then again, you might not.

When the cremeux is spoonable, get a spoonful of it and put it in your mouth. Spend the next few minutes contemplating life. What have you achieved today? How are you going to spend your remaining years? What's better, cheese on toast or cheese on its own? When you're done with that, spoon the rest of the cremeux on top of the pie and shmear it out so that it looks nice. Then add the chopped hazelnuts and you're done. Keep in the fridge and eat within 3 days.

ITALIAN MERINGUE

MAKES

MAKES

Approx. 500g (1lb 2oz), or enough to top a Lemon Meringue Pie (see page 58)

If we were caught up in some extremely bizarre set of circumstances that resulted in me asking you to close your eyes and think about meringue, your first thought would be how do I get out of this hellhole, but – ultimately – you'd almost certainly conjure up thoughts of a baked, colourless, soft but chewy sweet thing that you've eaten countless times throughout your life thus far on planet earth.

That's French meringue. There's nothing wrong with French meringue, in fact I happen to quite like it, but it's got nothing, I repeat nothing, on Italian meringue.

When made properly, the texture of Italian meringue is like nothing else (apart from imaginary, cartoon-style clouds) and it carries additional flavours with such grace and decorum. In theory it's a super-simple recipe, but in actuality, it requires some skill and in the wrong hands you'll be stood there looking into a bowl of soupy mess. Nobody wants that. So, do us all a favour and follow the recipe properly, would you? P.S. You're going to need a stand mixer for this recipe. I wouldn't attempt it without one, because your arm will probably fall off.

INGREDIENTS

475g (1lb ½oz) caster (superfine) sugar
160g (5½oz) cold water
260g (9¼oz) egg whites
1 tsp vanilla extract

METHOD

Put the caster (superfine) sugar and water in a heavy-bottomed saucepan and set to one side.

Fat residue will stop your egg whites from properly aerating, so it's crucial to ensure that both your stand mixer bowl and whisk are spotlessly clean. Wiping them down with vinegar or lemon juice is a firm favourite of pastry chefs, but I think it's unnecessary to be honest. Just make sure they're clean and you'll be good to go. By the way, egg yolk contains fat, so when you're separating your eggs you need to be extra careful to make sure that you don't get any yolk in your whites. If you do, you're going to need to start again. Add the egg whites to the clean stand mixer bowl and attach the whisk attachment.

Give the sugar and water a good stir, just enough to make sure that there's no sugar stuck to the bottom of the pan and place over a medium heat. Put a candy thermometer or temperature probe into the pan and, very importantly, don't leave the pan unattended.

Do not stir the mixture once you have put it onto the heat, just leave it to do its thing. When the sugar syrup reaches 115°C (240°F), turn your stand mixer onto the highest speed and begin whipping your egg whites. In the next couple of seconds your sugar is going to reach 120°C (250°F) and as soon as it does you need to remove the pan from the heat, turn the stand mixer down to low speed and slowly and steadily pour the sugar syrup into the egg whites.

The trick is to make sure that your egg whites are just at the soft peak stage at the point you pour in your sugar syrup. This is where skill and experience come in – it's like a juggling act between the eggs and the sugar. If the sugar takes longer than normal to reach 120°C (250°F) then you'll overwhip your egg whites and your meringue will be foamy as opposed to fluffy. If your eggs are under-whipped when you add your sugar syrup, then they'll never really whip enough and you won't get to experience the sensational pillowy-cloudlike mouthfeel of a properly made Italian meringue.

When pouring the sugar syrup, make sure that you pour it down the inside edge of the bowl and not directly onto the whisk, because the last thing you need is boiling sugar being flung around the kitchen. No really, that's super dangerous, so please pour carefully.

When you've poured all of the sugar syrup into the egg whites, turn the stand mixer to the highest speed. The fate of your meringue is now in the hands of the gods. There's nothing more to do at this point other than watch as it gets fluffy, glossy and delicious.

After about 10 minutes of whipping, your stand mixer bowl will go from being hot to the touch to room temperature. When you can comfortably touch the bottom of the bowl, add your vanilla extract. Continue to whip for another minute, or until the vanilla is evenly distributed. Believe me when I tell you, you'll know whether or not you've nailed the meringue when you taste it. If it's enjoyable, you've done something wrong. If it's out-of-this-world and so smooth that you can't even feel it in your mouth, then congratulations and welcome to Nirvana.

Your Italian meringue is ready to use straight away, as a topping on a Campfire Pie (see page 14) or a Lemon Meringue Pie (see page 58), or just straight out of the bowl. Try it with some fresh, in-season strawberries and a glass of champagne. The strawberries are optional, the champagne is not.

Italian meringue is best consumed on the day it's made. If you're not using it straight away, store it in the fridge in an airtight container and consume within 24 hours.

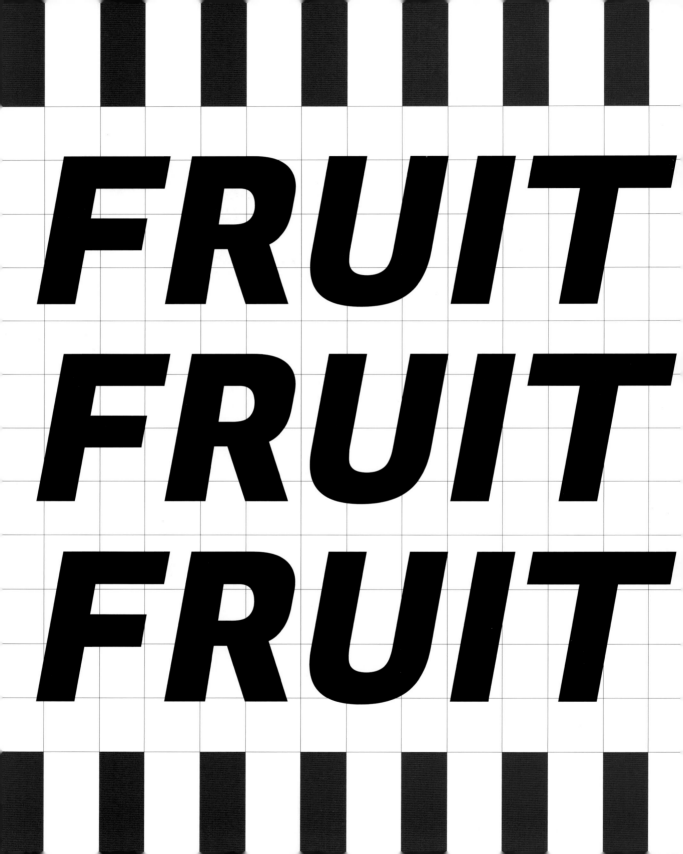

FRUIT
FRUIT FRUIT
FRUIT

LEMON MERINGUE PIE

SERVES

10–14

It's a classic, and I have to be honest with you, I think we do it very well at GET BAKED®. I am of the opinion that an LMP should be kept extremely simple, allowing the flavour combinations to do the talking, without any unnecessary fuss. Do me a favour and spend the money to get the best lemons you can find. The difference it makes to anything you're cooking when you use a better-quality acid is phenomenal, and this is especially the case with lemons.

You'll want to prepare your pie in advance, because the lemon posset will take a few hours to set, so bear this in mind before you get all excited. Don't worry though, you can do the meringue bit right before you serve it and that's the fun part anyway.

INGREDIENTS

For the toasted waffle crust

250g (9oz) shop-bought
  Belgian waffles
250g (9oz) oat biscuits
5g (⅛oz) sea salt
300g (10½oz) unsalted butter, cubed

For the lemon posset

800g (1lb 12oz) double (heavy) cream
200g (7oz) caster (superfine) sugar
80g (2¾oz) light brown sugar
grated zest and juice of 4 lemons

For the Italian meringue

500g (1lb 2oz) Italian meringue
  (page 52)

METHOD

Preheat your oven to 180°C (350°F/gas 4).

Blitz the Belgian waffles to a fine crumb in a food processor (or put them in a bag and bash them with a rolling pin). Once you've pulverised the living daylights out of them, spread the crumbs out on a baking tray and toast in the oven for 15 minutes or until they've browned slightly and your kitchen smells utterly sensational. While your waffle crumb is in the oven, pulverise the oat biscuits and decant them into a mixing bowl. Add your toasted waffle crumb and sea salt to the bowl and give everything a mix.

Put your butter in a heatproof, microwave-safe container. Microwave for about 1 minute 30 seconds, or until it's totally melted. Add the melted butter to your bowl of crumbs and mix thoroughly with your hands, ensuring an even distribution of melted butter. You don't want any dry patches, not now, not ever.

Press the mixture into a 30cm (12in) pie tin straight away, while the mixture is still warm. If you leave it too long, the butter will set and it'll become much less pliable. Make sure the crumb covers the base and sides of the tin. If you like, you can make the crumb mixture in advance, then just reheat the crumb in the microwave in short 15-second blasts.

Once you've lined your tin, bang it in the fridge to firm up. Ten minutes later it's ready to fill. If you're that way inclined, you can make your pie crust in advance and freeze it. It'll be good in the freezer for up to a month and won't lose any quality whatsoever.

→

Now onto the lemon posset. It's super simple, and hardly anything can go wrong, so relax and enjoy the ride. Heat the cream in a heavy-bottomed saucepan over a medium heat, stirring continually so that it doesn't catch and burn at the bottom. After a few minutes, or when the cream is starting to get warm enough to take an extremely relaxing bath in, add the sugars, lemon juice and zest to the pan and continue to stir.

Bring the cream to a simmer, but don't let it boil. Continue stirring and let it do its thing for a few minutes, adjusting the heat accordingly so that it doesn't get too hot, then take it off the heat. You want to make sure that the sugar has completely dissolved, which it should have done, but you can check by rubbing a small amount of the mixture between your fingers. Be careful, obviously. I don't need another lawsuit on my hands.

Pour the posset directly into the toasted waffle crust. If you've followed the measurements correctly, your crust should be about two-thirds full, which for me is the perfect ratio. If you have some posset left over, you can go rogue and fill it all the way to the top, I really don't care. If you're boring you can use less posset, resulting in a thinner pie, but if you've bought this book and that's your intention, you've probably made a mistake and should question everything about your life thus far.

Let it come to room temperature and then bang the pie in the fridge. It'll need to stay there for a few hours, until the posset is set. Your work here is done, and all there is to do now is adorn your baby with heaps of the good stuff (Italian meringue).

Follow the recipe for Italian meringue on page 52 and, using a spatula or a spoon (or your divorce papers), wallop dollops of meringue all over your pie. It'll look more professional if you're neat enough to not get any of it on the edges of the pie crust, but who cares about being professional – I don't and look how far I've come. I've changed my mind, get it all over the edges, get it everywhere, smear it on the worktop for no reason whatsoever. Go wild.

When your LMP is suitably festooned with meringue, borrow a blowtorch from your father-in-law and toast it right up (the pie, not your father-in-law).

PINK GRAPEFRUIT BARS

MAKES
10–16 bars

It's really important to use real grapefruit juice, not from a carton. I realise that squeezing this much fresh grapefruit juice sounds ridiculous, but if it's not freshly squeezed it just won't taste anywhere near as good.

INGREDIENTS

For the shortbread

375g (13oz) plain (all-purpose) flour, sifted
250g (9oz) unsalted butter, melted
125g (4¼oz) caster (superfine) sugar
5g (⅛oz) sea salt
5g (⅛oz) vanilla extract

For the pink grapefruit topping

450g (1lb) eggs
600g (1lb 5oz) caster (superfine) sugar
450g (1lb) pink grapefruit juice, freshly squeezed (2 or 3 grapefruits)
Pink food colouring (use as suggested on packaging)
70g (2½oz) plain (all-purpose) flour, sifted

To finish

Icing (powdered) sugar, for dusting

METHOD

Preheat the oven to 160°C (320°F/gas 3).

To make the shortbread base, all you've got to do is mix all of the ingredients in a mixing bowl until they come together and form a dough. The dough shouldn't be at all sticky, and it shouldn't stick to your hands, but if it does just mix through a little more plain (all-purpose) flour. Press the dough evenly into a 23 x 30cm (9 x 12in) baking tin lined with greaseproof paper. Bake in the oven for about 20 minutes or until the edges have started to turn golden.

While the shortbread is baking, make the pink grapefruit topping. Add the eggs, sugar and pink grapefruit juice to a mixing bowl and whisk until combined. Add pink food colouring (the amount will depend on the brand of colouring that you've got). Unfortunately, the juice from pink grapefruit isn't very pink, especially after you've baked it, and it's kind of underwhelming to serve a pink grapefruit bar that isn't pink. Next, add the flour and combine until incorporated. The mixture should be very thin, liquidy and smooth.

When the shortbread is baked, remove it from the oven and immediately poke holes all over it using a fork. This will allow the grapefruit to penetrate (oh yes) the shortbread so that it goes all gooey. Leave to cool slightly for 10 minutes, then pour the grapefruit mixture directly on top and put it back in the oven for another 20 minutes or until the top is just about set. If you tap the tin then a very slight jiggle in the centre is what you're looking for – only the hint, almost a memory of a jiggle. That's how faint we're talking. Leave to cool at room temperature for about an hour, then put in the fridge to chill and firm up for at least another 2 hours. Once they are firm, remove from the tin and slice into as many bars as you want. These bars are best served chilled, straight from the fridge. To finish, top them with a generous dusting of icing (powdered) sugar.

They'll keep for up to a week in an airtight container in the fridge, or for up to a month in the freezer. They're surprisingly delicious straight from the freezer. I'd give them about 15 minutes at room temperature first, but it sounded better to say straight from the freezer.

BANOFFEE PIE

SERVES

10–14

And here it is. The one and only. Banoffee Pie. The most popular pie on the menu at GET BAKED®, and for good reason. Our customers always want to know what we do to make it so good, and the secret is the banana custard. It's the almost artificial, overly-banana-like banana flavour that you get from the milkshake powder. It instantly takes you back to your childhood, and that's the secret behind our Banoffee Pie, and the secret behind most food that you love to eat and can't work out why. Nostalgia.

INGREDIENTS

For the biscuit crust

350g (12oz) oat biscuits
350g (12oz) digestive biscuits
350g (12oz) unsalted butter, cubed

For the caramel

600g (1lb 5oz) Caramel (see page 102)

For the banana custard

120g (4¼oz) double (heavy) cream
120g (4¼oz) whole milk
40g (1½oz) caster
  (superfine) sugar
75g (2¾oz) banana milkshake
  powder
2 egg yolks
1 ripe banana

For the whipped cream

500g (1lb 2oz) Properly
  Whipped Cream (see page 84)

To finish

25g (1oz) 55–70% dark chocolate

METHOD

Blitz the oat and digestive biscuits to a fine crumb in a food processor (or pop them in a bag and pulverise the living daylights out of them with a rolling pin). Transfer them into a mixing bowl.

Put your butter in a heatproof, microwave-safe container. Microwave for about 1 minute 30 seconds, or until it's totally melted. Add the melted butter to your bowl of crumbs and mix thoroughly, ensuring even distribution of melted butter so there are no dry patches. Press the mixture into your 30cm (12in) pie tin straight away, while the mixture is still warm and pliable. If you like, you can make the crumb mixture in advance, then just reheat the crumb in the microwave in short 15-second blasts.

Once you've lined your tin, bang it in the fridge for 10 minutes to firm up. Now it's ready to fill. If you're that way inclined, you can make your pie crust in advance and freeze it. It'll be good in the freezer for up to a month and won't lose any quality whatsoever.

The first layer of the pie is the caramel. Follow the recipe on page 102 and pour the caramel directly onto the chilled biscuit crust. Be careful because the caramel will be very hot. If you prefer, you can wait until the caramel has started to cool and thicken, then spoon it on rather than pour it. For the perfect finish when you slice the pie though, it's best to pour when hot. Bang it in the fridge to set for about an hour, or until the caramel doesn't wobble when you shake the tin but is still soft to touch.

While the caramel is setting, make the banana custard. Heat your milk and cream together gently in a heavy-bottomed saucepan over a low heat. Stir occasionally to avoid it catching at the bottom of the pan. While this is heating, whisk your sugar and milkshake powder into your egg yolks for a few minutes, until the yolk turns pale

and aerates slightly. The milkshake powder will contain cornflour (cornstarch), which will help thicken and set the custard; it's almost as if it was meant to be. When the milk and cream mixture is just beginning to bubble, pour a small amount into your eggs and sugar. This is to 'temper' the eggs and avoid them scrambling, which would be likely to happen if you just poured them into the cream.

Whisk the small amount of cream into the eggs and then pour the mixture back into the pan. Keep the heat low and switch to a heatproof spatula to mix your custard. It will thicken as it cooks, and you want to thicken it as much as possible, while being careful not to burn any at the bottom of the pan. The best way to stop this from happening is to stir the custard properly, obviously.

Once thickened, transfer the custard to a heatproof container and leave to cool at room temperature, directly covering the surface of the custard with cling film (plastic wrap) so that it doesn't form a skin. While your custard is cooling, peel and thinly slice the banana, then gently press the slices into the caramel. Pressing them in means that they won't be sliding all over the place when you add the custard. Clever. When your custard has cooled, spoon it all over the banana-topped caramel layer and spread it out evenly using a palette knife or the back of a spoon. After you've added the custard, put the pie back in the fridge to chill for at least 30 minutes, or until the custard is fridge-cold.

All that's left to do now is add your Properly Whipped Cream (see page 84). At GET BAKED®, we completely cover the custard with the cream, but there's nothing stopping you from leaving the edges exposed so that you can see the yellow of the custard. Either way, don't spread it too neatly because you want to see some texture from the cream. Finish by finely grating the dark chocolate on top of the cream: you'll hardly taste it, but it looks good.

The pie is ready to slice and serve straight away, or will keep perfectly in the fridge for up to 3 days. If you're going to freeze it, it's best to do this before you've added the cream. It will keep in the freezer for up to a month.

CARROT CAKE COOKIES

MAKES
10 cookies

It's just occurred to me that carrots aren't a fruit, and they're in the fruit chapter. Problem is, we don't have a vegetable chapter, and we can't make one just for this cookie. Please join me in momentarily pretending that carrots are a fruit. To be fair, they are one of your five-a-day and they're orange. So yeah, carrots.

INGREDIENTS

140g (5oz) softened
  unsalted butter
110g (3¾oz) caster (superfine)
  sugar
140g (5oz) light brown sugar
1 tsp vanilla extract
1 egg
140g (5oz) plain (all-purpose) flour,
  sifted
140g (5oz) strong white bread flour,
  sifted
1 tsp baking powder
1 tsp bicarbonate of soda
  (baking soda)
1 tsp sea salt
55g (2oz) freshly grated carrot
1 tsp ground cinnamon
½ tsp ground nutmeg
80g (2¾oz) roughly chopped pecans

For the cream cheese glaze
200g (7oz) icing (powdered) sugar
30g (1oz) maple syrup
30g (1oz) cream cheese
1 tsp vanilla extract

METHOD

Cream the butter and sugars together in the bowl of a stand mixer fitted with the beater attachment until pale and fluffy. Add the vanilla to your egg, then add to the butter and sugar mixture. Mix for 1 minute or until emulsified, then scrape down the base and sides of the bowl. Weigh out the flours, baking powder, bicarbonate of soda (baking soda), salt, grated carrot, cinnamon, nutmeg and chopped pecans and add to the bowl. Beat on the lowest speed until the mixture comes together.

Using an ice cream scoop or your hands, scoop the mixture into ten 100g (3½oz) pucks and place onto a greaseproof paper-lined tray. The mixture will feel quite sloppy because there's a lot of moisture in the carrot. This is normal and it gives the cookies a softer texture than our other cookies once baked. Cover the tray in cling film (plastic wrap) and put it into the fridge for at least 24 hours (at most 72 hours). If you absolutely must bake the cookies on the same day, try to give them at least 6 hours to chill before baking.

When you're ready to bake, preheat your oven to 150°C (300°F/gas 2). Split the 10 pucks across two greaseproof paper-lined baking trays, leaving enough space between them to allow for spreading in the oven. Bake for 12–15 minutes, or until the cookies resemble cookies. If they're still bulging in the centre, then they're not ready yet. Remove from the oven and leave to cool on the baking trays.

While your cookies are cooling, prepare the cream cheese glaze by whisking the icing (powdered) sugar, soft cheese, water and vanilla extract in a small mixing bowl.

When the cookies are cool, paint the glaze all over the cookies with a pastry brush, then set to one side to dry. The cookies will keep for up to two days in an airtight container at room temperature, but are best eaten the day you make them.

PURPLE HAZE PIE

SERVES
10–14

If you're one of those weirdos who's really into fruity desserts, this one's going to knock your socks clean off. If you're not, your socks will remain very much in-situ, but at least your feet will be warm.

INGREDIENTS

For the ginger biscuit crust

700g (1lb 9oz) ginger biscuits
400g (14oz) unsalted butter, cubed
5g (⅛oz) sea salt

For the lemon posset

800g (1lb 12oz) double
  (heavy) cream
200g (7oz) caster
  (superfine) sugar
80g (2¾oz) light brown sugar
grated zest and juice of 4 lemons

For the blueberry jam

700g (1lb 9oz) fresh blueberries
450g (1lb) granulated sugar
juice of 1 lemon
1 tbsp liquid pectin
  (available from your
  favourite online retailer)

METHOD

To make the ginger biscuit crust, turn your ginger biscuits into a fine crumb. Ideally, you'd use a food processor, or blender, but if you don't have either of those a bag and a rolling pin will do the trick. I once bashed some digestives using a bottle of wine, but let's not get into that. Once your biscuits are pulverised, add them to a mixing bowl.

Microwave the butter in a microwave-safe container until fully melted. Add the melted butter to the bowl of biscuit crumbs and mix together thoroughly using your hands. It's important to make sure that the butter is evenly distributed throughout the mixture. If the mix is feeling a little dry, melt another 50g (1¾oz) of butter and add a tablespoon at a time until you reach the desired consistency. You're looking for wet sand. Press the ginger biscuit crust into a 30cm (12in) pie tin, lining the base and the sides.

For the lemon posset, follow the exact recipe and method as used in the Lemon Meringue Pie (see page 58). Fill the crust with your posset mixture and leave to cool at room temperature. Once cool, bang it in the fridge for at least 6 hours, or until it's set. Ideally, overnight is best.

The blueberry jam is easy as pie, but not quite as easy as it was for me to come up with that horrendous pun. Put all of the ingredients in a heavy-bottomed saucepan and place over a medium heat. Using a potato masher, lightly squash the blueberries – just a gentle press is enough, it's nice to leave some whole. Give everything a good stir and bring to the boil. As soon as it's bubbling, turn the heat down low and simmer for 45 minutes, stirring occasionally with a heatproof spatula.

Take off the heat and decant into a heatproof container to cool. Once cool, spoon the jam on top of the set lemon posset layer. Don't pile it all into the middle or the weight of it might be too much for the lemon layer to contend with. Use a small offset palette knife or the back of a spoon to evenly spread the jam all over the pie, being careful not to cover the edges of the crust. Place the finished pie in the fridge for a few hours so that the jam can fully cool. It sounds silly, but it eats a lot better if you give the jam time to settle on top of the posset. Eat within 3 days, or keep in the freezer for up to a month.

STRAWBERRY LIMEADE PIE

SERVES
10–14

I'll be totally honest with you, we created this pie out of necessity. We had loads of limes to use up, and even more strawberries. This thing tastes exactly the same as a Twister ice lolly, which every British person knows is one of the greatest things that exists.

Just imagine. British summer. 28 degrees. Kids in the paddling pool. Gary's on the frozen margaritas. You're stuck in the kitchen boiling limes over a hot stove. Absolute, unadulterated bliss.

INGREDIENTS

For the ginger biscuit crust
700g (1lb 9oz) ginger biscuits
400g (14oz) unsalted butter, cubed
5g (⅛oz) sea salt

For the lime posset
800g (1lb 12oz) double (heavy) cream
200g (7oz) caster (superfine) sugar
80g (2¾oz) light brown sugar
grated zest and juice of 5 limes

For the strawberry jam
600g (1lb 5oz) fresh strawberries
350g (12oz) granulated sugar
juice of 1 lemon
1 tbsp liquid pectin
   (available from your
   favourite online retailer)

METHOD

To make the ginger biscuit crust, turn your ginger biscuits into a fine crumb using a food processor or blender (or a bag and a rolling pin). Once your biscuits are pulverised, add them to a mixing bowl.

Microwave the butter in a microwave-safe container until fully melted. Add it to the bowl of biscuit crumbs and mix together thoroughly using your hands, making sure that there are no dry patches. If the mix feels a little dry, melt another 50g (1¾oz) of butter and add a tablespoon at a time until you reach the desired consistency. You're looking for wet sand. Press the ginger biscuit crust into a 30cm (12in) pie tin, lining the base and the sides.

For the lime posset, follow the method as used in the Lemon Meringue Pie (see page 58), replacing the four lemons with five limes. Fill the crust with your posset mixture and leave to cool at room temperature. Once cool, bang it in the fridge for at least 6 hours or until it's set. Ideally, overnight is best.

For the strawberry jam, all you've got to do is put all of the ingredients into a heavy-bottomed saucepan and place it over a medium heat. Give them a stir and bring to the boil. As soon as the pan looks like a bubbling strawberry-laden party of chaos, turn the heat down to low and simmer for 45 minutes, stirring occasionally with a heatproof spatula.

Take off the heat and decant into a heatproof container to cool. Once cool, spoon the jam on top of the set lime posset layer, being careful not to pile it all into the middle. Use a small offset palette knife or the back of a spoon to evenly spread the jam all over the pie, making sure not to cover the edges of the crust. Place the finished pie in the fridge for a few hours so that the jam can fully cool and settle on top of the posset. Eat within 3 days, or keep in the freezer for up to a month.

HONEY PEACH PIE

SERVES

10–14

Thyme works extremely well with peaches and imparts a very subtle floral note. To be honest, you probably won't taste it, but sometimes it's just nice going to bed knowing that you're the sort of person who puts thyme on their honey-roasted peaches.

INGREDIENTS

For the honey-roasted peaches

400g (14oz) tinned peach halves, drained (the peaches, and also me, of any emotion)
150g (5½oz) runny honey
1 tsp sea salt
1 sprig of fresh thyme
250g (9oz) Caramel (see page 102)

For the amaretti biscuit crust

500g (1lb 2oz) amaretti biscuits
200g (7oz) oat biscuits
5g (⅛oz) sea salt
350g (12oz) unsalted butter, cubed

For the mascarpone cream

400g (14oz) double (heavy) cream
200g (7oz) mascarpone cheese
10g (¼oz) vanilla extract

To finish

30g (1oz) toasted flaked almonds

METHOD

Start with the peaches because they'll take a while to cook. Preheat your oven to 180°C (350°F/gas 4), then add your peaches, flat side down, to a baking tray. Drizzle evenly with honey and add the sea salt and the sprig of thyme. Cover the peaches with foil and prick some holes in it with a fork. Roast for 1 hour, then remove the foil and give them another 20 minutes to allow them to caramelise and turn an exquisite golden colour. After 20 minutes, remove the peaches from the oven and allow to cool. Once cool, decant them into a bowl. At this point, you can stir the thyme into the peaches and, all jokes aside, doing so will add a really nice floral note to the peaches.

Now onto the crust. Blitz the amaretti, oat biscuits and salt in a food processor to a fine crumb (or bash them with a rolling pin). Decant into a bowl. Put your butter in a heatproof, microwave-safe container. Microwave for about 1 minute 30 seconds, or until it's totally melted. Add the melted butter to your bowl of crumbs and mix thoroughly, ensuring even distribution of melted butter. Press the mixture into your 30cm (12in) pie tin straight away. Once you've lined your tin, put it in the fridge for 10 minutes to firm up.

For the caramel, follow the recipe on page 102. Once made, allow to cool at room temperature for 30 minutes before using. If you use it straight away, it will melt the butter in your biscuit crust and make a right mess. When the caramel has cooled, but is still liquid, pour it directly onto your biscuit crust. Top immediately with the peaches so that the peaches stick to the warm caramel. Place into the fridge to chill for 30 minutes or so.

For the mascarpone cream, add the double (heavy) cream and mascarpone to the bowl of a stand mixer fitted with the whisk attachment and whip together, following the principles for Properly Whipped Cream on page 84. Use an offset palette knife or the back of a spoon to evenly spread the mascarpone cream on top of the pie. Finish by adding the toasted almonds around the edge. As the pie contains cheese and fresh cream, it'll need to be kept in the fridge and eaten within 3 days.

BARBECUED BANANA BROWNIES

MAKES

10–16 slices, depends how big you want 'em

One of my fondest memories growing up was having barbecues. They didn't happen very often, and they weren't really very good, but there was something about them that I loved. After we'd eaten some overcooked burgers and undercooked sausages, my dad would throw some bananas on the barbecue.

I can still smell the banana juices dripping into the coals, as the scorched skin turned all kinds of black. After half an hour, they'd come off and we'd eat them with cheap vanilla ice cream.

INGREDIENTS

For the brownie

750g (1lb 10oz) caster (superfine) sugar
300g (10½oz) light brown sugar
520g (1lb 2½oz) 55% dark chocolate
520g (1lb 2½oz) unsalted butter, plus extra for greasing
460g (1lb ¼oz) eggs
380g (13½oz) plain (all-purpose) flour, sifted
140g (5oz) cocoa powder, sifted
5g (⅛oz) sea salt

For the caramelised pecans

150g (5½oz) pecan halves
25g (1oz) dark brown sugar
25g (1oz) honey

For the barbecued banana ganache

130g (4½oz) double (heavy) cream
400g (14oz) white chocolate (chopped up if in bar form)
50g (1¾oz) banana milkshake powder
10g (¼oz) smoked sea salt

METHOD

Follow the recipe for the O.G. Brownies (see page 18) and slice your brownies into 10–16 slices using a sharp cook's knife.

To make the caramelised pecans, preheat your oven to 150°C (300°F/gas 2), then toss the pecan halves in the dark brown sugar and honey in a mixing bowl until they're evenly coated. Bake in the oven on a parchment-lined baking tray for 20 minutes, or until the pecans look shiny. Remove from the oven and set aside to cool.

Now for the banana ganache. Combine the double (heavy) cream, white chocolate and banana milkshake powder in a heavy-bottomed saucepan and place over a very low heat, stirring continuously with a heatproof spatula. The ganache will split extremely easily if you overheat it, so take it off the heat every 30 seconds so that it doesn't get too hot. Keep stirring, making sure that the chocolate is always in motion, especially around the sides and bottom of the pan. Take the pan off the heat when there are still a few chunks of white chocolate left; you can stir out the remaining bits of chocolate while off the hob.

Pour the ganache into a 5cm (2in)-deep tray to set. You're not going to be dipping your brownies in it, you're going to be letting it set enough so that it's spreadable. You can speed up the process by putting the ganache in the fridge. When the ganache has a chocolate spread sort of texture, it's ready to use. You're going to be topping the flat underside of your brownies, using a small palette knife to spread a generous schmear of ganache all over your brownies. You can make it neat if you like, but personally I think messiness adds to the charm.

Now add a couple of caramelised pecans and a pinch of smoked sea salt. Go easy on the salt or your brownie will end up tasting like a medium-rare steak. Not ideal.

BAKED CHERRY AND CUSTARD CRUMBLE PIE

SERVES

10–14

Don't make the cherry element of this pie because it won't be as good. You want that classic, almost fake-tasting cherry taste and you just won't get that if you use fresh cherries. This pie is nostalgic. I demand nostalgia. Also, take my advice and eat it warm.

INGREDIENTS

750g (1lb 10oz) shop-bought cherry pie filling

For the pastry

140g (5oz) unsalted butter, softened
60g (2¼oz) icing (powdered) sugar
25g (1oz) egg
275g (9¾oz) plain (all-purpose) flour, sifted
5g (⅛oz) sea salt
15g (½oz) cold water

For the custard

600g (1lb 5oz) double (heavy) cream
600g (1lb 5oz) whole milk
8 large egg yolks
30g (1oz) cornflour (cornstarch)
5g (⅛oz) vanilla extract
120g (4¼oz) caster (superfine) sugar
1 gelatine sheet

For the spiced crumble

150g (5½oz) plain (all-purpose) flour, sifted
75g (2¾oz) soft light brown sugar
75g (2¾oz) oats
1 tsp ground cinnamon
½ tsp ground nutmeg
100g (3½oz) cold butter

METHOD

To make the pastry, beat the softened butter and icing (powdered) sugar in a stand mixer fitted with the paddle attachment until light and fluffy. Add the egg and beat on low speed for about 30 seconds. Scrape down the bowl, ensuring there's no butter stuck to the bottom or sides, and continue to beat on low speed until the egg is combined. Add the flour, salt and water and mix until only just combined. Do not overmix the dough or it'll be ruined. The dough will be in ruins. Have you been to Pompeii? Wrap the dough in cling film (plastic wrap) and refrigerate for at least 30 minutes before using.

When chilled, roll out the dough on a floured work surface using a rolling pin, to a thickness of about ½cm (¼in) and bang the pastry into a 30cm (12in) pie dish. Tidy the edges using a paring knife and prick holes all over the bottom of the base. About 10 should do it. Put it back in the fridge to chill. Just so you know, it'll keep perfectly well in the fridge for up to 3 days if it's wrapped in cling film, and up to 1 month in the freezer. We use this recipe for any and all of our sweet pie crusts.

For the custard, gently heat your double (heavy) cream and milk in a heavy-bottomed saucepan until just boiling. Stir occasionally to avoid it catching on the bottom of the pan. Meanwhile, in a mixing bowl, whisk the eggs with the cornflour (cornstarch), vanilla extract and sugar, until pale. Add the hot cream and milk to the bowl one ladle at a time, whisking well after each addition. When you've finished adding all of the milky cream, or creamy milk, pour it back into the pan, and cook over a low heat, whisking continually, for about 25 minutes, or until thickened.

Meanwhile, soak the gelatine sheet in cold water for 2 minutes to soften it. Take the pan of custard off the heat, then squeeze out the water from the gelatine and add it to the thickened custard, whisking thoroughly to combine. Allow to cool at room temperature while you preheat the oven and get on with making your spiced crumble.

GET BAKED

→ Preheat your oven to 160°C (320°F/gas 3).

To make the spiced crumble mix, put the flour, sugar, oats, cinnamon and nutmeg in the bowl of a stand mixer fitted with the paddle attachment. Chop the cold butter into cubes and add it to the bowl. Mix on a medium speed until the butter is evenly distributed: the mixture should be crumbly and not stuck together. If it's stuck together, the butter wasn't cold enough. To make sure this doesn't happen, just leave the butter in the fridge right up until you need it – you can even freeze it for 30 minutes beforehand if you're bored and just looking for unnecessary things to do.

When the custard has cooled down slightly, spoon it into the pastry case and spread it out evenly using the back of a spoon. Bake in the oven for 15 minutes, then remove from the oven and add the cherry pie filling. For the record, I love tinned pie filling. It's exactly the taste that you want, in the same way that sometimes tinned fruit is just perfect for certain recipes. I'm totally comfortable in telling you that we don't make our own cherry pie filling at GET BAKED®, because it would cost far too much money, take far too much time and wouldn't achieve the flavour profile that we're going for. For me, I don't want a cherry pie filling that tastes like fresh cherries. I want a cherry pie filling that tastes like my childhood. When you've added the pie filling, sprinkle the crumble mixture evenly all over the top, and return to the oven to bake for a further 15 minutes.

You'll know it's ready because your kitchen will smell fantastic, and the crumble will be golden brown. As tempting as it might be to slice and eat it straight away, you really need to allow it to cool for at least 30 minutes. Weirdly enough, to experience it at its best, you should let it chill overnight, then slice it the next day. Heat each slice in the microwave for around 30 seconds if you'd prefer it warm, which in my opinion is definitely best.

I don't know the science behind why the pie is better the next day, and I'm not going to pretend to – I just know after making lots of them that it's the case.

The pie will be good for up to 3 days in the fridge.

BLUEBERRY PANCAKE COOKIES

MAKES
10 cookies

It's like sitting down to breakfast in an American sitcom from 1993. But it isn't an American sitcom and it isn't 1993. That's how good this recipe is – you won't even know what year it is.

INGREDIENTS

140g (5oz) softened unsalted butter
110g (3¾oz) caster (superfine) sugar
140g (5oz) light brown sugar
1 tsp vanilla extract
1 egg
140g (5oz) plain (all-purpose) flour, sifted
140g (5oz) strong white bread flour, sifted
1 tsp baking powder
1 tsp bicarbonate of soda (baking soda)
1 tsp sea salt
120g (4¼oz) fresh blueberries

For the maple glaze

200g (7oz) icing (powdered) sugar
50g (1¾oz) maple syrup

METHOD

Cream the butter and sugars together in the bowl of a stand mixer fitted with the beater attachment until pale and fluffy. Add the vanilla to your egg, then add to the butter and sugar mixture. Mix for 1 minute, or until emulsified, then scrape down the base and sides of the bowl. Weigh out the flours, baking powder, bicarbonate of soda (baking soda) and salt, and add to the bowl and beat on the lowest speed until the mixture comes together.

Using an ice cream scoop, or your hands, scoop the mixture into ten 100g (3½oz) pucks and place onto a greaseproof paper-lined tray. Carefully press the blueberries into the pucks, doing your best not to squish them. You'll more than likely suffer some casualties, but their injury will only add to the flavour and general blueberry-like aesthetic of the cookies, so it's not all bad. Cover the tray in cling film (plastic wrap) and put it into the fridge for at least 24 hours (at most 72 hours). If you absolutely must bake the cookies on the same day, try to give them at least 6 hours to chill before baking.

When you're ready to bake, preheat your oven to 150°C (300°F/gas 2). Split the 10 pucks across two greaseproof paper-lined baking trays, leaving enough space between them to allow for spreading in the oven. Our cookies are quite thin, they're a classic, crispy on the edges, chewy on the outside and soft in the middle type of affair.

Bake for 12–15 minutes. If the cookies are still bulging in the centre, then they're not ready yet. Remove from the oven and leave to cool on the baking trays.

While your cookies are cooling, prepare the maple glaze by whisking the icing (powdered) sugar and maple syrup together in a small mixing bowl.

When the cookies are cool, paint the glaze all over the cookies using a pastry brush, then set to one side to dry. The cookies are best eaten the day you make them, but will keep for up to 2 days at room temperature in an airtight container.

PROPERLY WHIPPED CREAM

MAKES

Approx. 500g (1lb 2oz),
or enough to top 1 Banoffee Pie
(see page 64)

I know what you're thinking. You think you already know how to whip cream. You're wrong. You don't know how to whip cream. You know how to overwhip cream. If you're using a stand mixer, or even a hand mixer, I'm pretty sure you're overwhipping your cream.

It sounds totally ridiculous, but we were three months deep into opening GET BAKED® before we realised that we couldn't even whip cream properly and now I'm writing a recipe book. Con man, genius, or both – you decide. Anyway, back to the cream fiasco, yeah you don't know what you're doing.

You'll notice that there's no sugar in our whipped cream. This might seem a bit strange, but I am totally against using sugar in cream. Everything we make is sweet, and the cream is there to calm things down, give an unctuous mouthfeel and make everything else stand out.

500g (1lb 2oz) double (heavy) cream
5g (⅛oz) vanilla extract
 (the better, the better)

Basically, if you're mixing cream using a stand mixer fitted with the whisk attachment, which most home bakers are, you need to turn the machine off well before you've actually reached whipped cream consistency.

Add the vanilla to the cream at the very beginning and turn the machine on to a medium-high speed. The key is to turn the machine off as soon as you notice the cream getting more aerated. This is nowhere near 'whipped cream' consistency, it'll just look lighter in texture with a few small air bubbles. At this point, remove the bowl from the mixer and, using the whisk attachment, whisk the mixture by hand. The problem with using your stand mixer to whip cream is that the cream collects on the whisk in the centre of the bowl and overwhips. Even though the cream looks fine, it isn't because the middle has been overwhipped.

It's still best to use a stand mixer to begin with, because it's a lot quicker, and whisking double (heavy) cream by hand is just exhausting and far too much exercise. From experience, the cream will be perfect when it's at a point that you think is just slightly under-whipped. When you think it's done, it's actually ruined. The difference between cream that's been perfectly whipped and cream that's overwhipped is momentous. The texture is totally different, it's not claggy, it's perfectly light and almost non-existent.

You could say that properly whipped cream is almost invisible to the palette, and you'd only recognise it if it wasn't there. Maybe I'm overthinking it, but we whip a ridiculous amount of cream, and this is the sort of state you find yourself in when you're me. I dunno.

Stop whipping cream to the point where it looks like it's come out of a can. It's a sin.

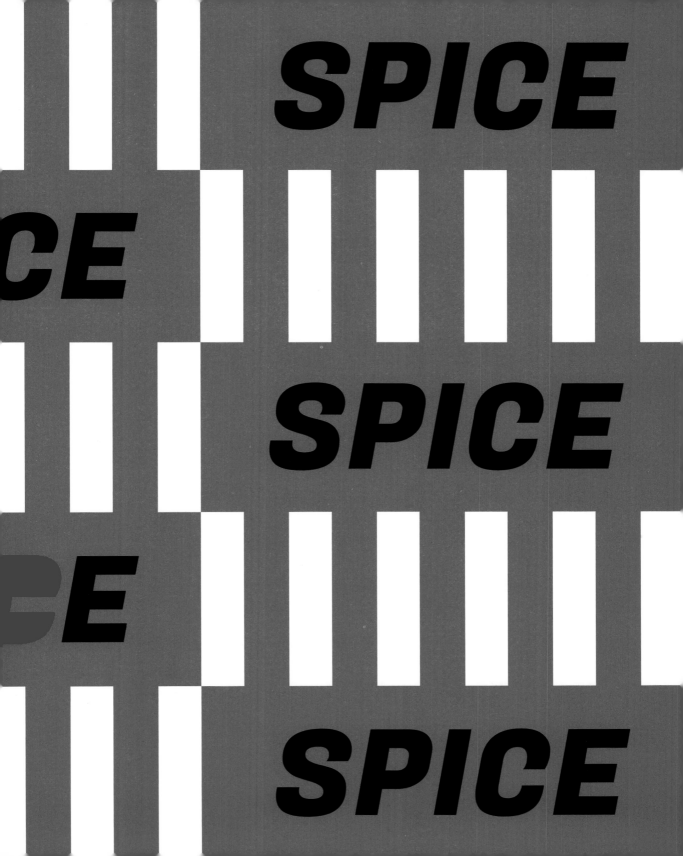

MORNING BUNS

MAKES

6 buns

This isn't my recipe, and I don't even care. My good friend, the incredibly talented pastry chef and owner of Fluff Bake Bar in Houston, Texas, Rebecca Masson, gave it to me.

She makes insanely good cinnamon buns, and I made some with her when I was doing a pop-up at her place. I said to her, 'I'm just letting you know that these are going to have to go in my book, because they're absolutely sensational.' She agreed, so here we are.

The great thing is, they're actually totally uncomplicated. It's just about knowing when the dough is right, which comes with a bit of experience. Even if you don't absolutely nail it, they'll still taste amazing.

The only slight change I made to her recipe is the addition of brown sugar in the filling. She doesn't think it needs it. I do. I win.

INGREDIENTS

For the dough

350g (12oz) plain (all-purpose) flour, plus extra for dusting
120g (4¼oz) whole milk
70g (2½oz) caster (superfine) sugar
60g (2¼oz) softened unsalted butter, plus extra for greasing
10g (¼oz) dried active yeast
5g (⅛oz) sea salt

For the filling

100g (3½oz) softened unsalted butter
15g (½oz) ground cinnamon
50g (1¾oz) dark brown sugar

For the frosting

100g (3½oz) icing (powdered) sugar, sifted
100g (3½oz) cream cheese
50g (1¾oz) unsalted butter, cubed
50g (1¾oz) whole milk
5g (⅛oz) vanilla extract

METHOD

To make the dough, put all of the ingredients in the bowl of a stand mixer fitted with the dough hook attachment and mix on a slow-medium speed for 6 minutes, or until the dough is pulling away from the sides of the bowl. You can do this by hand, but honestly, why would you want to do that? You're not Paul Hollywood. And even if you were, you'd still use the dough hook.

At this point, stop kneading and pull the dough out. Place the dough into the largest mixing bowl you've got (lightly greased with a very small amount of flavourless oil), cover it with a slightly damp tea towel and put it somewhere warm to prove. You're looking for the dough to double in size, which will take at least an hour.

When your dough looks puffy as hell, dust your worktop with flour and – using a rolling pin, or a bottle of Robinson's fruit cordial (honestly, I've seen it happen) – roll the dough out to a thickness of 1cm (½in), doing your best to keep it rectangular in shape. This can be tricky, but just manipulate the edges by pushing them to form the desired shape – this takes a bit of getting used to, but you'll get there, maybe.

Now, in a mixing bowl, combine the ingredients for the filling and shmear them evenly all over your dough, leaving a 2.5cm (1in) gap around the edges of the dough.

GET BAKED

Using your fingers, roll up the dough tightly from the edge nearest you, as evenly as you can muster. Take your time with this bit: it's not a race. Relax and enjoy the roll. You're rolling and nobody can stop you. It's empowering. Anyway, make sure you roll it quite tightly or your buns will all but completely unravel when they're in the oven.

Once rolled, slice off the edges, because they'll be lacking in filling, and cut your log into six even rolls. Shmear some butter around the bottom and edges of a 23cm (9in) cake tin (7.5cm/3in deep) and carefully place your rolls into the tin, with five around the sides and one in the middle. The middle one will be the ultimate roll, and you mustn't let anyone else eat that one. That is yours.

Cover the tin with the same tea towel as before and place it somewhere warm again, until they've yet again doubled in size (this will take at least 30 minutes). I realise there's a lot of leaving-somewhere-warm-to-double-in-size going on here, but that's just kinda the way it is.

Once they've doubled in size, they're finally ready to go in the oven. Preheat your oven to 150°C (300°F/gas 2).

Bake the buns for 12–15 minutes. They'll be golden brown on top, but check they're cooked in the middle by carefully pulling the edge of one of the rolls away and inspecting the consistency of the dough. They should be light, fluffy, springy and dense. Like me, but less tasty.

I like to make the frosting now rather than in advance. I prefer to frost the buns when they're slightly warm, but not hot, otherwise it melts everywhere and doesn't look as good. To make the frosting you just need to combine all of the ingredients in the bowl of a stand mixer using the beater attachment. Beat on medium-high speed for 5 minutes or until the mixture is smooth and spreadable.

When the buns have cooled down but are still slightly warm to the touch, remove from the tin and cover the living daylights out of them with the frosting. Less is not more.

Break them apart, or serve as a tear-and-share sort of situation. Alternatively, serve as a whole, and forget the share bit.

Cinnamon buns have a notoriously short shelf-life, and if you want to experience them at their best, you really need to eat them on the day they're made. If you have to, you can store them in an airtight container at room temperature and eat the next day, but they won't be quite the same. However, if you give them 10–15 seconds in the microwave to soften, they won't be far off.

CINNAMON TOASTER PASTRIES

MAKES
8 pastries

As the recipe states, please don't actually put these in your toaster. The glaze will melt and the whole thing will end in tears. They are only called 'toaster pastries' because it means you can eat them for breakfast. I'm just looking after your best interests.

INGREDIENTS

For the pastry
550g (1lb 4oz) softened unsalted butter
260g (9¼oz) icing (powdered) sugar
100g (3½oz) eggs (plus approx. 50g/1¾oz extra for egg wash)
1kg (2lb 4oz) plain (all-purpose) flour, plus extra for dusting
60g (2¼oz) cold water
5g (⅛oz) sea salt

For the filling
100g (3½oz) soft light brown sugar
5g (⅛oz) plain (all-purpose) flour
10g (¼oz) ground cinnamon
5g (⅛oz) sea salt

For the glaze
200g (7oz) icing (powdered) sugar, sifted
75g (2¾oz) whole milk
5g (⅛oz) vanilla extract
pinch of ground cinnamon

METHOD

Start by making the pastry dough. Beat the butter and icing (powdered) sugar together in the bowl of a stand mixer fitted with the beater attachment until pale and fluffy. Add the egg and continue to mix until incorporated. Scrape down the base and sides of the bowl and beat further. It's essentially just a load of beating. Add the flour, water and salt, and you guessed it, beat. Mix until it just about comes together, then form it into a ball. Wrap in cling film (plastic wrap) and chill in the fridge for at least an hour. Chilling the dough will make it much easier to work with.

After an hour take the dough out of the fridge and lightly dust a clean worktop with flour. Weigh the dough and divide it in half. Roll half of the dough out to a thickness of roughly 3mm (⅛in), trying your best to form it into a rectangle. This is quite difficult to do and to be perfectly honest I'm terrible at it. Just sort of work the edges of the dough with the rolling pin, pushing it into a rectangular shape. It's manipulation. You're manipulating your ingredients and I hope you're proud of yourself.

When you're done manipulating, cut the dough into 8 even rectangles. Use a ruler. Get scientific. Do some maths on a calculator. Put glasses on. Look clever. Ring your dad for advice. When you've got 8 rectangles, transfer them onto a lined baking tray and bang them back in the fridge so they can have a long hard think about what they've done. Just kidding – they're badly rolled rectangles not naughty children. Now do exactly the same with the other half of the dough. The reason you've done this in two sections is because have you ever tried to roll out enough dough to cut 16 rectangles? No, you haven't. Well, I have and let me tell you, it's carnage. Put the remaining 8 rectangles onto another lined baking tray and insert them into the fridge.

While the dough is chilling in the fridge, beat the remaining egg in a bowl and leave to one side, that's Mrs. Eggwash and shortly you will require her assistance. Preheat your oven to 180°C (350°F/gas 4).

→

Now get on with the filling. Combine the light brown sugar, flour and cinnamon in a bowl. That's literally it. It's nothing ground-breaking but it tastes nice, and that's all that matters. If you want complicated, build a flatpack wardrobe. After you've made the filling, take both trays of dough out of the fridge and brush eight of the rectangles with egg wash. To be clear, you're only brushing one side of them, not both. The egg wash will help the filling stick to the dough and it'll also help the other rectangle to stick on top. Use a spoon to add an even layer of the filling to the egg-washed rectangles, ensuring that you leave a gap around the edges so that the other rectangle will stick on top. Use the back of the spoon to flatten the filling, you want it to be quite compact, and the brown sugar will make this quite easy to do.

Assemble the toaster pastries by placing the spare rectangles on top of the filling-topped ones. Push down gently around the edge so that they stick together, and use a fork to crimp around the edges – this will help avoid any leakage. Brush the top of each pastry with egg wash and use the fork to poke a couple of small holes into each one. This will ensure that steam is able to be released from inside the pastry – if you don't do this, they'll probably explode. This has the potential to be a rather enjoyable spectacle to witness from the other side of the oven door, but just think of the mess. Bake for about 20 minutes, or until a light golden brown.

When baked, remove from the oven and leave to cool at room temperature while you make the vanilla glaze. The vanilla glaze is just as easy as the filling, you just need to combine the ingredients in a bowl. Mix until smooth – this can take a few minutes because there will be clumps of icing sugar. The glaze should be runny but not thin. Thick, but not too thick. Maybe it's not that simple after all. When the pastries are totally cool, brush or spoon the glaze over the top and leave to set. I've realised that they're called toaster pastries but whatever you do don't put them in the toaster. The glaze will melt and it'll probably break the toaster.

If you want to enjoy them warm, I'd recommend warming them in the microwave for about 15 seconds. They won't taste as good in 2 days' time, so enjoy them on the day they're made or the day after. They'll freeze really well and keep for up to a month in the freezer (just make sure you defrost them before heating them up in the microwave).

CINNAMON AND RAISIN COOKIES

MAKES
10 cookies

These are my favourite cookies in the whole wide world. Everything is just perfect. The combination of cinnamon with the caramel notes that you get from the brown sugar. And then the raisins. Oh my, the raisins. Why aren't we eating raisins more often? Let me know.

INGREDIENTS

140g (5oz) softened unsalted butter
110g (3¾oz) caster (superfine) sugar
140g (5oz) light brown sugar
1 tsp vanilla extract
1 egg
140g (5oz) plain (all-purpose) flour, sifted
140g (5oz) strong white bread flour, sifted
1 tsp baking powder
1 tsp bicarbonate of soda (baking soda)
1 tsp sea salt
1 tsp ground cinnamon
80g (2¾oz) raisins

For the vanilla glaze
200g (7oz) icing (powdered) sugar, sifted
30g (1oz) water
1 tsp vanilla extract

METHOD

Cream the butter and sugars together in the bowl of a stand mixer fitted with the beater attachment until pale and fluffy. Add the vanilla to your egg, then add to the butter and sugar mixture. Mix for 1 minute, or until emulsified, then scrape down the base and sides of the bowl. Weigh out the flours, baking powder, bicarbonate of soda (baking soda), salt, cinnamon and raisins, and add to the bowl. Beat on the lowest speed until the mixture comes together.

Using an ice cream scoop, or your hands, scoop the mixture into ten 100g (3½oz) pucks and place onto a greaseproof paper-lined tray. Cover the tray in cling film (plastic wrap) and put it into the fridge for at least 24 hours (at most 72 hours). If you absolutely must bake the cookies on the same day, try to give them at least 6 hours to chill before baking.

When you're ready to bake, preheat your oven to 150°C (300°F/gas 2). Split the 10 pucks across two greaseproof paper-lined baking trays, leaving enough space between them to allow for spreading in the oven. Our cookies are quite thin, crispy on the edges, chewy on the outside and soft in the middle.

Bake for 12–15 minutes, or until the cookies resemble cookies. If they're still bulging in the centre, then they're not ready yet. Remove from the oven and leave to cool on the baking trays.

While your cookies are cooling, prepare the vanilla glaze by whisking the icing (powdered) sugar, water and vanilla extract in a small mixing bowl.

When the cookies are cool, paint the glaze all over the cookies using a pastry brush, then set to one side to dry.

The cookies will keep for up to 2 days at room temperature in an airtight container, but are best eaten on the day you make them.

SPECULOOS PIE

SERVES

10–14

Nobody knows exactly how a little Belgian biscuit has managed to slowly take over the world over the last decade, but it's impossible to refute the reality of the situation we have found ourselves in. They're everywhere. Never mind artificial intelligence, it's the caramelised biscuit you should be worried about.

INGREDIENTS

For the caramelised biscuit crust

700g (1lb 9oz) Lotus biscuits
5g (⅛oz) sea salt
400g (14oz) unsalted butter, cubed

For the caramel

600g (1lb 5oz) Caramel (see page 102)
1 tsp ground cinnamon
½ tsp ground nutmeg

For the Lotus Biscoff cream

450g (1lb) Lotus Biscoff spread
400g (14oz) double (heavy) cream
1 tsp vanilla extract

To finish

25g (1oz) Lotus biscuits, crushed

METHOD

Blitz the Lotus biscuits and salt in a food processor to a fine crumb, then decant into a mixing bowl. Melt your butter in the microwave in a heatproof, microwave-safe container until it's totally melted. About 1 minute 30 seconds should do it. Add the melted butter to your bowl of crumbs and mix thoroughly, ensuring even distribution of melted butter. Press the mixture into your 30cm (12in) pie tin straight away, while the mixture is still warm. If you leave it too long, the butter will set and it'll become much less pliable. If you like, you can make this in advance, then just reheat the crumb in the microwave in short 15-second blasts.

Once you've lined your tin, bang it in the fridge to firm up. Ten minutes later it's ready to fill. If you're that way inclined, you can make your pie crust in advance and freeze it. It'll be good in the freezer for up to a month and won't lose any quality whatsoever.

Now get on with making the caramel from page 102. As soon as you take the caramel off the heat, stir in the cinnamon and nutmeg. This is your spiced caramel. Let it cool at room temperature for up to 30 minutes before pouring into the biscuit crust, otherwise it'll be so hot that it'll melt the butter in the biscuits and you'll have a real situation on your hands.

Melt 400g (14oz) of the Lotus Biscoff spread in the microwave and pour it directly onto the caramel layer. You should do this while the caramel is still warm because it'll help the spread stick to it. If the caramel is cold when you pour the melted spread over it, the layers won't bond as well and the pie might come apart when you slice it. When melted, the Biscoff spread should be pretty thin, but just in case it hasn't covered the whole pie, use the back of a spoon to even it all out. Bang it in the fridge to set for at least 30 minutes.

Make Properly Whipped Cream using the double (heavy) cream and vanilla extract, following the method on page 84. Top the pie with the cream and melt the remaining 50g (1¾oz) of Lotus Biscoff spread

→

in the microwave. When melted, pour it all over the cream. There won't be enough to cover the cream, it'll just be a sort of Jackson Pollock splattering. Use an offset palette knife, or the back of a spoon, to shmear the Biscoff spread into the cream, but don't mix it in – you don't want brown cream, you want cream-coloured cream with caramel-coloured swirls. It's hard to explain. Work it out. Top the pie with the 25g (1oz) of crushed Lotus biscuits for added crunch, as the textures of this pie are all pretty soft. There's nothing wrong with soft though really – everybody likes a bit of soft from time to time.

Keep refrigerated and consume this pie within 3 days (although I really doubt it will last that long, because it's absolutely delicious).

CARAMEL

MAKES

Approx. 600g (1lb 5oz), or enough
to top one Banoffee Pie
(see page 64)

I very much enjoy making a caramel: it's just one of those things that every budding baker or pastry aficionado should know how to do, because it's so versatile, and a starting point for so many other recipes. The thought of making your own caramel can be a bit intimidating, but in reality, it's a breeze. Not only is it easy enough for even the most beginner bakers to pull off, it'll keep for up to a month in the fridge and up to three months in the freezer.

There are a few different ways to make it, and in my opinion, most of them are just unnecessarily complicated. My rule is simple. If you can use fewer ingredients, put them together simply, and get a great result, then do that. This works for baking, and for life in general. Baker or philosopher, I'll let you decide.

You're going to be working with very hot sugar, which can cause some very serious burns if it gets on your skin. So, remember to keep your wits about you, and use some common sense for a change.

On a side note, a lot of people ask me to explain the difference between caramel and butterscotch. To save you the time of getting your phone out and searching online, I'll tell you now. Caramel is made using white sugar, and butterscotch is made using brown sugar. You can have that one for free.

INGREDIENTS

350g (12oz) caster (superfine)
  sugar
70g (2½oz) water
200g (7oz) double (heavy) cream
90g (3¼oz) unsalted butter, cubed

METHOD

Put the sugar and water into a heavy-bottomed saucepan and stir the water into the sugar. Place over a medium heat and leave the sugar to dissolve. Do not stir, and don't be tempted to pick the pan up and mess around with it.

When the sugar has dissolved, the colour will start to change, starting off a pale yellow, and eventually turning to a deep amber. The trick to good caramel is knowing how far to take the sugar. If you don't get to the deep amber stage, and you add the cream and butter, your caramel will be underwhelming. If you take it too far, you'll burn the sugar and the caramel will be bitter and laden with bits of burnt sugar. Not good.

When your sugar is bubbling aggressively and has a deep amber colour, remove from the heat and carefully add the double (heavy) cream. Be very careful, because the cold cream is going to shock the caramel and cause it to bubble even more aggressively. Immediately stir the cream into the sugar using a heatproof silicone spatula. Once the bubbling has settled down, add the butter and continue to stir until the butter has melted.

The mixture should now resemble caramel, but don't taste it yet because it'll be hotter than the sun. At this stage, you could add a pinch of good-quality sea salt (welcome to 2010, you've got salted caramel). The mixture will still be quite thin because caramel thickens as it cools. Pour into a heatproof container and leave to cool at room temperature.

Once cool, you can store the caramel in the fridge for up to one month, or in the freezer for up to three months. When the caramel is cold, it'll set very firm, so to loosen the caramel for use, heat it in the microwave in 20-second bursts (or in a heavy-bottomed saucepan over a low heat) until it has reached the desired consistency.

SUGAR

SUGAR

SUGAR

SUGAR

SUGAR

SUGAR

EDIBLE COOKIE DOUGH

MAKES

24 pucks

You can have some fun with this one and add something else is well as (or instead of) the chocolate. Roasted peanuts are a nice addition – although I particularly enjoy replacing the chocolate with a bit of cinnamon and a handful of raisins. But then again, I am old and very boring.

INGREDIENTS

320g (11¼oz) plain (all-purpose) flour
300g (10½oz) dark chocolate,
  chopped up if in bar form
420g (15oz) softened unsalted butter
230g (8oz) caster (superfine) sugar
460g (16oz) light brown sugar
5g (⅛oz) sea salt
70g (2½oz) double (heavy) cream
10g (¼oz) vanilla extract

METHOD

Preheat your oven to 180°C (350°F/gas 4).

Start by baking the flour for 15 minutes. Just bang it all onto a baking tray as evenly as possible, and you're good. This step is really important because raw flour can contain some harmful bacteria that you don't want to eat – baking it will kill 'em dead. When baked, leave to cool at room temperature.

If you've got dark chocolate chips then you're good to go, but if your chocolate is in bar form, chop it up into small chunks. Cream the softened butter, sugars and salt in the bowl of a stand mixer fitted with the beater attachment until light and fluffy. Scrape down the base and sides of the bowl, then add the cream, vanilla and chocolate and continue to beat for another minute or until incorporated.

Once the flour has cooled, add it to the cookie mixture and beat until mixed thoroughly. Your cookie dough is now ready. It's as easy as that. What a breeze. You can do whatever the hell you want with it. Try it with some good-quality vanilla ice cream, or just eat it with a spoon – I quite literally don't care.

Keep refrigerated and eat within 3 days (unless you've gone through it all in one night, in which case I'd consider contacting your local health department). The cookie dough will also keep in the freezer for up to a month.

RASPBERRY-GLAZED DONUT COOKIES

MAKES
10 cookies

The cookie that catapulted us into viral stardom. Once outlawed due to the use of illegal sprinkles, now made possible once more thanks to our very own brand. Don't scrimp on the sprinkles. Not now, not ever.

INGREDIENTS

140g (5oz) softened
  unsalted butter
110g (3¾oz) caster (superfine) sugar
140g (5oz) light brown sugar
1 tsp vanilla extract
1 egg
140g (5oz) plain (all-purpose) flour,
  sifted
140g (5oz) strong white bread flour,
  sifted
1 tsp baking powder
1 tsp bicarbonate of soda
  (baking soda)
1 tsp sea salt

For the raspberry donut glaze

200g (7oz) icing (powdered) sugar
30g (1oz) water
raspberry flavouring
  (use as instructed on packaging)

To finish

100g (3½oz) expen$ive sprinkles

METHOD

Cream the butter and sugars together in the bowl of a stand mixer fitted with the beater attachment until pale. Add the vanilla to your egg, and then add to the butter and sugar mixture. Mix for 1 minute, or until emulsified, then scrape down the base and sides of the bowl. Weigh out the flours, baking powder, bicarbonate of soda (baking soda) and salt and add to the bowl. Beat on the lowest speed until the mixture comes together.

Using an ice cream scoop, or your hands, scoop the mixture into ten 100g (3½oz) pucks and place onto a greaseproof paper-lined tray. Cover the tray in cling film (plastic wrap) and put it into the fridge for at least 24 hours (at most 72 hours). If you absolutely must bake the cookies on the same day, try to give them at least 6 hours to chill before baking.

When you're ready to bake, preheat your oven to 150°C (300°F/gas 2). Split the ten pucks across two greaseproof paper-lined baking trays, leaving enough space between them to allow for spreading in the oven.

Bake for 12–15 minutes, or until the cookies resemble cookies. If they're still bulging in the centre, then they're not ready yet. Remove from the oven and leave to cool on the baking trays.

While your cookies are cooling, prepare the raspberry glaze by whisking the icing (powdered) sugar, water and raspberry flavouring in a small mixing bowl. Take your time, and mix thoroughly, to ensure that you don't end up with any clumps of unmixed icing sugar – biting into that is the worst thing ever. Well, not the worst thing ever but it's pretty annoying.

While the glaze is still wet and the cookies have cooled, use a pastry brush (or the back of a spoon if you're ill prepared) to paint the glaze all over your cookies. Adorn your donut-inspired cookies straight away with lots of sprinkles and set to one side to dry.

The cookies will keep for up to 2 days in an airtight container at room temperature, but are best eaten the day you make them.

MILK & COOKIES CHEESECAKE

SERVES
10–14

You can buy cookies & cream spread from supermarkets and online retailers. There is no point whatsoever trying to make it yourself. The ones that you can buy are everything you'd hope they'd be: overly sweet, unhealthy and delicious.

INGREDIENTS

For the Oreo cookie crust

1.2kg (2lb 12oz) Oreo cookies
350g (12oz) unsalted butter, cubed
400g (14oz) cookies & cream spread

For the Oreo cheesecake

670g (1lb 8oz) full-fat cream cheese, at room temperature
135g (4¾oz) double (heavy) cream
120g (4¼oz) icing (powdered) sugar
170g (5¾oz) white chocolate, chopped up if in bar form
105g (3½oz/1 pack) Oreo cookies

For the topping

400g (14oz) Properly Whipped Cream (see page 84)
20g (¾oz) Oreo cookies, blitzed to a crumb

METHOD

Start by making the Oreo cookie crust. Blitz the Oreo cookies in a food processor or with a rolling pin to a fine crumb, then decant into a mixing bowl. Melt your butter in the microwave in a microwave-safe container until it's totally melted (about 1 minute 30 seconds). Add the melted butter to your bowl of crumbs and mix thoroughly. Line your 30cm (12in) pie tin with the mixture straight away, then bang it in the fridge to firm up. Ten minutes later it's ready to fill.

Melt the cookies & cream spread in the jar or tub in the microwave – ensuring you remove any foil – and pour directly into your Oreo cookie crust. Spread evenly with a palette knife or the back of a spoon. Bang it in the fridge to chill while you move onto the next stage of the pie.

In the mixing bowl of a stand mixer fitted with the whisk attachment, mix the cream cheese and double (heavy) cream together, beating on medium speed for exactly 2 minutes, then turn the mixer speed to the lowest setting and slowly add the icing (powdered) sugar. Don't add it all at once because it'll go everywhere and gets in your nose, which is unpleasant in every way imaginable. When you've added all of the sugar, keep the speed on the lowest setting and continue to beat while you melt your white chocolate. Microwave it in short bursts, stirring in between. When melted fully, pour into your cheesecake mixture and continue to beat. Turn the speed back up to medium for a few seconds and then scrape down the base and sides, focusing on the base – it's likely that there will be some cheese down there that hasn't mixed in properly. Add the pack of crushed Oreo cookies and give it another 30 seconds on the highest speed.

Spoon the cheesecake mixture into your chilled pie crust and spread it out evenly. Bang it back in the fridge to set for at least 3 hours. It needs to set fully to be experienced at its best, otherwise it can be a bit sloppy. After it's set, finish the pie by topping it with Properly Whipped Cream (see page 84). Adorn your creation with the small amount of crushed Oreo cookies that you have left.

Serve from the fridge (it's a cheesecake you loser) and enjoy within 3 days. I wouldn't freeze it. You could but just don't.

EXPEN$IVE BUNS

MAKES

6 buns

What's better than cinnamon buns? Nothing. What's on par? These.

These are essentially cinnamon buns for people that don't like cinnamon, but love fluffy, dense and indulgent baked dough. We replace the sharp, cinnamon-enriched filling with an amazing sandy birthday-cake crumble which, when baked, goes all kinds of gooey.The way the sprinkle-laden sand cooks inside the dough, providing a super moist filling, is honestly something to behold.

INGREDIENTS

For the dough

350g (12oz) plain (all-purpose) flour, plus extra for dusting
120g (4¼oz) whole milk
70g (2½oz) caster (superfine) sugar
60g (2¼oz) softened unsalted butter, plus extra for greasing
10g (¼oz) dried active yeast
5g (⅛oz) sea salt

For the expen$ive filling

85g (3oz) plain (all-purpose) flour
75g (2¾oz) caster (superfine) sugar
45g (1½oz) cold butter, cubed
10g (¼oz) custard powder
1 tsp vanilla extract
1 tsp sea salt
40g (1½oz) expen$ive sprinkles, plus extra to finish

For the glaze

100g (3½oz) icing (powdered) sugar
25g (1oz) softened unsalted butter
50g (1¾oz) whole milk
1 tsp vanilla extract

METHOD

To make the dough, combine all of the ingredients in the bowl of a stand mixer fitted with the dough hook attachment and mix on a slow-medium speed for 6 minutes, or until the dough is pulling away from the sides of the bowl. You can do this by hand, but honestly why would you want to do that.

Place the dough in the largest mixing bowl you've got, cover it with a slightly damp tea towel and put it somewhere warm to prove. You're looking for the dough to double in size, which will happen in anywhere from 3 to 6 hours.

When your dough looks puffy as hell, dust your worktop with flour and roll out the dough to a thickness of 1cm (½in), doing your best to keep it rectangular in shape, manipulating the edges by pushing them to form the desired shape – this bit takes a bit of getting used to, but you'll get there, maybe.

Now, combine all the ingredients for the expen$ive filling – apart from the sprinkles – in the bowl of a stand mixer fitted with the beater attachment. Add the sprinkles by hand at the end, just because you don't want them to get pulverised. The mixture will resemble a fine, sandy crumb, very similar to a crumble mix that you'd shove on top of a pie. Once sandy crumb status has been achieved, sprinkle it all over the dough, leaving a 2.5cm (1in) gap around the edge of the rectangle of dough. Once covered, use your hands to press the crumb down, so that it's nice and compact. This is essential, so don't forget to do it.

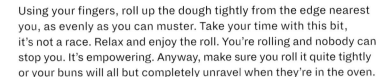

Using your fingers, roll up the dough tightly from the edge nearest you, as evenly as you can muster. Take your time with this bit, it's not a race. Relax and enjoy the roll. You're rolling and nobody can stop you. It's empowering. Anyway, make sure you roll it quite tightly or your buns will all but completely unravel when they're in the oven.

Once rolled, slice off the edges, because they'll be lacking in filling, and cut your log into six even rolls. Shmear some butter around the bottom and edges of a 23cm (9in) cake tin (7.5cm/3in deep) and carefully place your rolls into the tin, with five around the sides and one in the middle. The middle one will be the ultimate roll, and you mustn't let anyone else eat that one. That is yours.

Cover the tin with the same tea towel as before and place somewhere warm again, until they've yet again doubled in size. I realise there's a lot of leaving-somewhere-warm-to-double-in-size going on here, but that's just kinda the way it is.

Once they've doubled in size, they're finally ready to go in the oven. Preheat your oven to 150°C (300°F/gas 2).

Bake the buns for 12–15 minutes. They'll be golden brown on top, but check they're cooked in the middle by carefully pulling the edge of one of the rolls away and inspecting the consistency of the dough. They should be light, fluffy, springy, and dense. Like me, but less tasty.

I like to make the glaze now rather than in advance. I prefer to frost the buns when they're slightly warm, but not hot, otherwise it melts everywhere and doesn't look as good.

To make the glaze, just combine all of the ingredients in the bowl of a stand mixer fitted with the beater attachment and beat on medium-high speed for 5 minutes or until the mixture is smooth and spreadable.

When the buns have cooled down but are still slightly warm to the touch, remove from the tin and cover the living daylights out of them with the glaze. Less is not more. Finish with a generous helping of expen$ive sprinkles for extra ridiculousness.

Break them apart, or serve as a tear-and-share sort of situation. Alternatively, serve as a whole and forget the share bit.

These buns have a notoriously short shelf-life and if you want to experience them at their best, you really need to eat them on the day they're made. If you have to, you can store them in an airtight container at room temperature and eat the next day, but they won't be quite the same. However, if you give them 10–15 seconds in the microwave to soften, they won't be far off.

EXPEN$IVE BIRTHDAY CAKE

SERVES
10–40

I hate to sound like I'm coercing you into buying my sprinkles, but they really are the only way to achieve the desired aesthetic here. All other sprinkles that look this good are illegal in the UK.

INGREDIENTS

For the funfetti sponge

1.25kg (2lb 12oz) margarine (this is the only recipe where I advocate using it)
1.25kg (2lb 12oz) caster (superfine) sugar
1.25kg (2lb 12oz) eggs (approx. 25 eggs)
10g (¼oz) vanilla extract
1.25kg (2lb 12oz) self-raising flour, sifted
10g (¼oz) sea salt
100g (3½oz) expen$ive sprinkles

For the vanilla buttercream

1kg (2lb 4oz) softened unsalted butter
1.75kg (3lb 13oz) icing (powdered) sugar, sifted
50g (1¾oz) custard powder
50g (1¾oz) whole milk
10g (¼oz) vanilla extract

To finish

500g (1lb 2oz) expen$ive sprinkles
The ability to re-mortgage after spending all of your money on sprinkles

METHOD

Preheat your oven to 160°C (320°F/gas 3).

To make the sponge, cream the margarine and caster sugar in the bowl of a stand mixer (using the paddle attachment) until light and fluffy. This will take at least five minutes on a high speed. Add the eggs five at a time (if you add them all at once, the mixture will split). Once the mixture looks smooth, add five more eggs, then repeat the process until you've added all of the eggs. Add the vanilla extract with the last five. When you're out of eggs, scrape down the bowl and continue to mix for another minute. Then scrape down the bowl again – I know this seems like overkill but it's worth it – continue to beat for another minute and then add the flour in three stages, beating between each addition so that it's totally incorporated. When you've added all of the flour, add the salt and the sprinkles and give a final mix using a spatula or wooden spoon.

Line the base and sides of three 23cm (9in) round baking tins (7½cm/3in deep), then split the mixture evenly between them. Give the tins a firm bang on the workbench to knock out any large air bubbles, they'll ruin your life later on when you're trying to slice the sponges, so this is very important. Bake for an hour or until they're golden brown on top and a skewer comes out totally clean. When baked, leave to cool at room temperature inside the tins. After about half an hour, remove the cake from the tins and continue to cool at room temperature.

When they're totally cool, they're ready to slice. You're going to be slicing each sponge into four thin layers, so you'll end up with a total of twelve. Slice the domed tops off and cling film (plastic wrap) them to make our Birthday Truffles (see page 120). Who wants to waste cake? I don't, that's for sure. Follow the instructions for slicing Bruce on page 129. When you've got twelve thin layers of sponge stacked on top of each other with a layer of greaseproof paper between them, wrap the stack in clingfilm and refrigerate. You want the sponge to be cold and firm when you're assembling the cake.

Whilst the sponges are firming up you can make your buttercream. In the bowl of a stand mixer, use the beater attachment to cream the

→ butter on high speed for at least five minutes, or until the butter is very pale. It should go from being yellow to almost white. Add the icing (powdered) sugar in stages and beat on high speed for at least a minute between each sugar addition. Add the custard powder, vanilla extract and milk in with the last load of sugar and continue to beat for at least another 10 minutes. This seems like a long time, but it's essential if you want to achieve a really smooth buttercream.

By now, your sponges should be nice and firm and you're ready to assemble your cake, following the instructions for assembling Bruce on pages 129–30. Once assembled, it's time to apply the crumb coat. This is a very thin layer of buttercream that goes all over your cake to lock in the crumbs and stop them from going into your buttercream when you coat the outside of the cake. If you don't apply one, it's not the end of the world, but you might find bits of sponge make their way into your buttercream. This can spoil the appearance and, more importantly, the texture. It doesn't need to look neat, it just needs to be smooth. When applied, place the cake into the fridge to set.

Once set, you can apply the rest of the buttercream all over your cake. Some people like to use a piping (pastry) bag, but personally I prefer to just use a palette knife. If you do want to use a piping bag, start at the bottom and pipe rings of buttercream all around the cake while turning the turntable. Then use a palette knife to shmear the buttercream around the cake, removing the excess in the process. Obviously, you can reuse the excess because there will be no crumbs in it. Thank you crumb coat, our lord and saviour. Repeat the process until your cake is covered and there are no uneven, buttercream-lacking crevices. Remember you're going to cover the entire cake in sprinkles, so it doesn't really matter if it's not smooth. If you'd rather just use a palette knife, follow exactly the same method but just shmear the buttercream on, rather than piping it. When your cake is covered, immediately coat the whole thing in expen$ive sprinkles. It's important that you apply the sprinkles before the buttercream has set too firmly, or the sprinkles won't stick properly. There's not really a way of doing this that won't result in sprinkles going all over the worktop, so just make sure it's clean so any stragglers can be collected and reapplied to the cake. When the cake is sufficiently covered, you're done.

I'd recommend putting it in the fridge for at least 30 minutes before slicing, just to ensure that the buttercream has set. In the unlikely event that you've got leftover cake, it'll keep perfectly fine in a sealed container for 3 days, or in the freezer for up to a month.

BIRTHDAY TRUFFLES

MAKES

24 truffles

These truffles make use of leftover funfetti sponge from the Expen$ive Birthday Cake. They are about half the size of Bruce's Balls, so you'll need to use a smaller ice cream scoop to get the right size.

INGREDIENTS

For the sprinkle sand

50g (1¾oz) custard powder
50g (1¾oz) plain (all-purpose) flour
15g (½oz) cornflour (cornstarch)
20g (¾oz) caster (superfine) sugar
20g (¾oz) expen$ive sprinkles
5g (⅛oz) sea salt
60g (2¼oz) unsalted butter, melted

For the insides

The tops from 3 funfetti sponges
  (see page 117)
150g (5½oz) whole milk

For the white chocolate coating

50g (1¾oz) white chocolate,
  chopped up if in bar form
25g (1oz) vegetable oil

METHOD

Preheat your oven to 140°C (275°F/gas 1).

Start by making the sprinkle sand. Combine all the dry ingredients in a bowl, then add the melted butter and toss with a spoon until evenly distributed. The mixture should start to come together, forming small clusters. Spread out on a greaseproof paper-lined baking tray and bake for 20 minutes. The texture should be totally dry at this point – if it's not, give it a few more minutes. When baked, leave to cool at room temperature, then blitz to a crumb in a food processor. You don't want it too fine; it's best to use the pulse setting on the processor. If there isn't one, you could use a rolling pin or, if you're at your grandma's house, a pestle and mortar.

Now onto the truffle's insides. Break the sponge into big pieces and put into the bowl of a stand mixer fitted with the beater attachment and beat the sponges on the lowest speed. When the sponges are broken and the contents of the bowl look like a cake crumb, add the milk, bit by bit. You might not need all the milk, just keep adding it until the cake comes together as one. The mixture should be easy to roll into balls without leaving any residue on your hands.

Using your ice cream scoop, scoop the cake into 24 truffles and use your hands to roll into balls. Place the truffles onto a lined baking tray and refrigerate so they firm up. While they're chilling, make the white chocolate coating. Melt the chocolate in the microwave, stirring between short bursts so that it doesn't burn. Once melted, thoroughly mix in the oil.

You're going to need someone to help you assemble the truffles. Wearing food-safe gloves, shmear some of the white chocolate onto the inside of your hands and roll the truffles in it, covering them in a thin layer of white chocolate. Toss the coated truffles into the sprinkle sand, so that your baking buddy (cringe) can cover them. Repeat the process until all of the truffles are coated.

It's tempting to eat them straight away, but you should put them in the fridge for 30 minutes to give the white chocolate a chance to set – it's just better, trust me. Keep them in the fridge and eat them within 3 days. They'll keep in the freezer for up to a month.

BRUCE

BR

BRUCE

BR

BRUCE

BRUCE

There's a common misconception that I'd like to address before I continue. Bruce is not named after a character from a popular children's book who was force-fed a very large chocolate cake. I have never read the book, nor seen the movie, and it is purely coincidental. An annoying coincidence, but a coincidence, nonetheless.

It's hard to know where to begin with introducing Bruce. I never thought I'd find myself in a position where I refer to a cake as 'he' without even thinking about it. It's because Bruce is so much more than just a chocolate cake – he's got more personality than most of the people I've crossed paths with in my life.

Customers visit our store from all over the world just to bag a slice of Bruce. I mean that quite literally. In August 2022 we also launched our nationwide delivery service, and highly specialised packaging has allowed us to put Bruce in the hands of people all over the country, with next day delivery. We sell 1,000 slices a week, and at the time of writing this book, we're yet to experience a day of trading where we haven't sold out.

I've been incredibly fortunate to have held pop-ups in both Houston and Austin, Texas, where the queues for Bruce stretched for so long that the fire department turned up to see what had happened. Nothing had happened, apart from the arrival of a 24-layer chocolate cake from Leeds. In case you're wondering, the fire department ended up staying, and they very much enjoyed themselves.

This book simply wouldn't have come into being if it wasn't for Bruce, and I wouldn't have been presented with anywhere near as many opportunities if it hadn't been for him.

When I told people that this recipe was going to be included in this book, they thought I was crazy, but nothing is going to fill me with more pride than seeing people attempt to make Bruce in their kitchen at home.

It's going to be complete and utter carnage, and I'm all for it.

For the dark chocolate sponge

780g (1lb 11oz) plain (all-purpose) flour, sifted
5g (⅛oz) sea salt
20g (¾oz) bicarbonate of soda (baking soda)
800g (1lb 12oz) unsalted butter
1.3kg (3lb) caster (superfine) sugar
450g (1lb) soured cream
350g (12oz) 55% dark chocolate, chopped up if in bar form
500g (1lb 2oz) water
600g (1lb 5oz) eggs (approx. 12 eggs)
220g (7¾oz) cocoa powder, sifted

For the dark chocolate ganache

3kg (6lb 8oz) 55% dark chocolate, chopped up if in bar form
3kg (6lb 8oz) double (heavy) cream

MAKING THE DARK CHOCOLATE SPONGE

Before you begin, get your mise en place in order by decanting everything into the correct vessel and arranging everything in one hell of an organised fashion. Plain flour, salt and bicarbonate of soda, together in a mixing bowl. Unsalted butter and caster sugar, together in your stand mixer's mixing bowl. Soured cream in a small bowl. Dark chocolate in a microwavable container. Water in a medium-sized saucepan. Eggs, cracked and in a mixing bowl. And finally, cocoa powder in a small bowl.

Using the beater attachment for your stand mixer, beat the butter and sugar together on a medium-high speed for at least five minutes, or until the mixture is pale and fluffy. You'll need to scrape the bowl down at least twice, to ensure that the butter and sugar are fully combined. Use a spatula.

While your butter and sugar are being beaten into oblivion, put the pan of water on to boil over a low-medium heat. Place the chocolate in the microwave for 30 seconds while the water is warming. Keep heating in 30-second bursts, ensuring that you stir thoroughly in between each burst. Once melted, set to one side.

When your water has come to a simmer, add in the cocoa powder, and whisk thoroughly using a hand whisk. Remove from the heat and continue to whisk until it forms a smooth paste. Add your melted chocolate to the pan, mix thoroughly, and set to one side.

Once the butter and sugar mixture is pale and fluffy, turn the speed to low and add your eggs four at a time. Continue to beat the mixture on low until the eggs are incorporated and everything has emulsified. Now add the soured cream along with the chocolate mixture and beat until incorporated. Finally, add the flour, bicarbonate of soda, and salt, and fold in on the slowest speed setting. Make sure there's no pockets of flour because it'll create all kinds of havoc when you put him on the oven. Your mixture should look smooth and glossy.

Line the base and sides of three 23cm (9in) round cake tins (7½cm /3in deep), then split the mixture evenly between them. Give the tins a firm bang on the workbench to knock out any large air bubbles.

Bake at 150°C (300°F/gas 2) for 60 minutes, or until a toothpick inserted into the centre of each cake comes out clean.

Once baked, leave to cool inside the tins and at room temperature for at least 2 hours. After 2 hours, remove the sponges from the tins, wrap in cling film (plastic wrap) and place in the fridge for at least another hour. Alternatively, you can wrap them in cling film and bang them in the freezer. They'll keep in there for up to 1 month and they freeze amazingly well. You'd never know they'd been frozen, it doesn't affect the quality of the cake whatsoever.

MAKING THE DARK CHOCOLATE GANACHE

Put the 3kg (6lb 8oz) of dark chocolate in a large, microwave-safe mixing bowl and heat the cream in a heavy-bottomed pan over a low heat, stirring continually so that it doesn't catch at the bottom of the pan. When the cream is hot, but not boiling, remove from the heat, and pour directly onto the chocolate. It's tempting to stir straight away, but if you do, you'll take too much heat out of the cream, and the chocolate might not all melt, so leave the mixture alone for 5 minutes. Then, use a heatproof spatula to combine the cream and chocolate. Keep stirring until the chocolate has melted and the mixture is smooth and glossy. If there are some pesky pieces of chocolate that just won't melt, place the bowl in the microwave and heat in 10-second bursts, stirring vigorously between each burst. Alternatively, place the bowl over a pan of simmering water and stir until the chocolate has melted – make sure the base of the bowl isn't touching the water. With either of these methods, it's important that you don't overheat the chocolate, as it'll split.

When the chocolate has melted and the ganache is smooth and glossy, add the sea salt and blend using a stick blender. If you don't have a stick blender, I would strongly recommend buying one. You can skip this step, but if you want perfectly smooth ganache, you really need to immersion-blend it. There will be tiny bits of chocolate that you can't see or even feel, and using a stick blender will pummel them into non-existence, resulting in a ganache that is so smooth you won't even know what day it is. It's Monday. Just kidding, I don't know what day it is either.

Blitz for at least 5 minutes, ensuring that you keep the blender submerged at all times, or you'll incorporate air into the ganache, and you don't want that. When you're done, cover the surface with cling film and leave to set at room temperature. It's tempting to speed up the process by putting in the fridge, but don't do this: the ganache around the edges of the bowl will set quicker than in the middle, and that will cause all sorts of chaos. At room temperature it's going to

take about 2 hours for your ganache to be set enough to use. This is just one of those things that you can't rush. It's worth bearing in mind that you don't want the ganache to be too well set either – if you leave it for too long, it'll be too hard to shmear, and you'll need to heat it up gently to soften it again. This is not what you want to happen – believe me. I have spent countless hours reheating ganache that was overset and it's an absolute nightmare. The consistency you're looking for is like Nutella. Spreadable, but not runny. Thick, but not so thick that it'll break your palette knife.

ASSEMBLING BRUCE

While your ganache is setting, slice the sponges. Each sponge will be sliced into four, so you'll have twelve all together. You can do this using a cake wire, but I've honestly never used one, so I can't give you any tips in that regard – but it's probably easier than doing it the way we do it at GET BAKED®. We do it with a very long serrated bread knife, and a turntable. Using the turntable to turn the cake, slice the sponge one layer at a time. It's a difficult technique to explain without showing you, but the way to achieve level slices is to let the knife do the work, keep your cutting hand (and the knife) still, and focussing your attention on turning the cake around the knife. The top of the cake will be slightly domed, uneven, and imperfect. Slice the tops off and cling-film them to use later. You won't need them for Bruce, but they'll be essential if you want to make Bruce's Balls (see page 133) – plus, who wants to waste cake. I don't, that's for sure.

When you've taken the top off, slice the cake into layers and stack them on top of each other with a layer of greaseproof paper between them so that they don't stick. When you've sliced all three cakes, removed all the tops, and got twelve thin layers of sponge, wrap the stack in cling film and put them back in the fridge.

You're now at the mercy of your ganache. You can't start to build Bruce until the ganache is set perfectly. Any attempts to start prematurely will end in tears. I've been there and it's hell.

When the ganache is ready, place a 28cm (11in) cake drum on top of your cake turntable (with a damp J-cloth underneath to stop it sliding) and place the first layer of sponge into the middle of the drum. It's very likely that you'll have some layers that are thicker than others, and I'd recommend using the thicker ones at the bottom of the cake. Think of them like foundations for building your house. Except you're not building a house, you're building one of the most famous chocolate cakes in the world. It's important to bear in mind

→

that Bruce is not supposed to be pretty. For that reason, I would only recommend using a palette knife to apply the ganache, and not a piping (pastry) bag. Piping bags are great if you want everything to look like it's been made by someone that knows what they're doing, but you don't know what you're doing, and that's fine.

Shmear a thick layer of ganache on top of your first layer of sponge, then repeat the process until you've reached the top. Stop every couple of layers to make sure that Bruce is straight – you can do this by eye, or by using a spirit level. I'd recommend using a spirit level, it might seem a bit over the top but the last thing you want is a 24-layer chocolate cake that looks like it is on the verge of collapse. You need to be quite quick when you're assembling Bruce, because the ganache will continue to set while he's being built. The last thing you want is to get to a point where your ganache is too firm, and you've got to soften it.

When you've built him, crack straight on with covering his exterior in ganache. Continue using a palette knife to encase him, and use a cake scraper to achieve a smooth finish. Bruce's signature lined pattern is achieved by warming a clean palette knife under a hot tap and turning the turntable around the palette knife, creating a sort of hypnotic whirl. Make sure you dry the palette knife after warming it, or you'll get water drops all over him, and he doesn't like water.

Bruce will be ready to slice immediately – he doesn't need any time to set, because he's Bruce, and he makes his own rules. You'll need a very large, very sharp, non-serrated knife. If you haven't got one, buy one, because everyone should have one in their kitchen. Make sure the knife is hot before you attempt any slicing – run it under a hot tap and dry it off with a towel. I'm going to be honest with you, slicing Bruce perfectly is not easy, and it takes most of our team about 200 slices worth of practice before they're able to slice him perfectly.

Slices of Bruce will keep perfectly well for up to 3 days in a sealed container. Some people seem to like to keep him in the fridge, but I strongly recommend storing Bruce at room temperature. You will not experience him at his best if he's fridge cold, so if you do insist on keeping him refrigerated, let him come up to room temperature before devouring him. He also freezes incredibly well for up to a month. Honestly, you'd never even know he'd been frozen.

Personally, I like to enjoy Bruce warm, but this is totally down to preference. At room temperature, he is obviously extremely rich and incredibly dense. After 20 seconds in the microwave, his ganache will soften, and he will just be easier to gorge on.

BRUCE'S BALLS

MAKES

12 Balls

INGREDIENTS

For the chocolate crumble

30g (1oz) water
100g (3½oz) caster (superfine) sugar
75g (2¾oz) 55% dark chocolate,
  chopped up if in bar form
5g (⅛oz) sea salt

For his insides

The tops from 3 Bruce sponges
  (see page 126)
150g (5½oz) whole milk

For the chocolate coating

50g (1¾oz) 55% dark chocolate,
  chopped up if in bar form
25g (1oz) vegetable oil

There's no better way to utilise your leftover Bruce sponge than to turn it into the most magnificent cake truffle you've ever tasted.

METHOD

Start by making the chocolate crumble. Heat the water and sugar in a saucepan over a medium heat. Using a candy thermometer or temperature probe, take the sugar syrup to 130°C (270°F). Do not stir or do anything at all with the pan. Be careful because these are extremely high temperatures and if you think burning yourself on an oven is bad, wait until you do it with boiling sugar – it's not fun. At all. As soon as it reaches temperature, remove from the heat and add the chocolate to the pan. Stir immediately using a wooden spoon. The chocolate crumble will form almost instantly as the chocolate seizes the sugar syrup and things just get very magical for a couple of seconds.

That's it, your chocolate crumble is ready; all you've got to do now is let it cool down for a few minutes before blitzing to a crumb in a food processor. When you've done that, set it to one side.

Now for the main element of Bruce's Balls – their insides. Break the sponges up into big pieces and put into the bowl of a stand mixer fitted with the beater attachment. Beat the sponges on the lowest speed. This is the easiest way to break the sponges up, if you try to do it by hand, the heat from your hands will make it more difficult. When the sponges are broken and the contents of the bowl look like a cake crumb, add the milk, bit by bit. You might not need all the milk, certain things will play a part in how much you need, for example, the heat in your kitchen and how well you baked the sponges. If you overbaked them, they'll be drier and will therefore require more milk. This also means you're a failure and I want nothing to do with you. Close the book. We're finished. Anyway, add the milk until the cake comes back together and forms a big ball of moistness. You don't want it to be wet, you want it to be moist. That's right. Moist. The mixture should be easy to roll into balls without leaving any residue on your hands. If cake is sticking to anything other than more cake, you've added too much milk. If you add too much milk, you'd better hope you've got some spare cake left to add to the mixture.

Bruce's Balls are big. They are not supposed to be the size of a chocolate truffle. If you want to make bitesize balls or baby balls (weird) then that's on you. However, Bruce's Balls are of a particular size and I'd appreciate

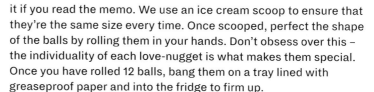

it if you read the memo. We use an ice cream scoop to ensure that they're the same size every time. Once scooped, perfect the shape of the balls by rolling them in your hands. Don't obsess over this – the individuality of each love-nugget is what makes them special. Once you have rolled 12 balls, bang them on a tray lined with greaseproof paper and into the fridge to firm up.

While they're getting firm, make the chocolate coating. This is just good-quality dark chocolate mixed with a flavourless oil. We use vegetable oil because it's readily available and doesn't taste like licking an olive. Melt the chocolate in the microwave in 30-second bursts, stirring between bursts so that it doesn't burn. Once melted, thoroughly mix in the oil. The oil stops the chocolate from setting. It's going to take a bit of time to coat the balls and if the chocolate didn't have any oil in it, it would start hardening while you were mid-flow. The oil keeps things slick. This is starting to sound like an erotic novel. It isn't, it's a recipe book. Bear in mind, the chocolate will still harden with the oil in it, it just takes longer – so you should still work pretty quickly.

The next part is a two-person job so you're going to have to rope someone in to help you. If you try and do it alone it's just really annoying. Maybe you could turn it into a team-building exercise at the workplace? Whatever the situation may be, you'll need a ball-rolling partner. One person is covering the balls in chocolate, and the other person is rolling them around in the chocolate crumble. I'd strongly recommend that the person covering the balls in the melted chocolate wears gloves, it's just a lot less messy. If you throw the balls in the chocolate, they'll get far too much chocolate on them. You only want a very thin layer of chocolate, as its main job is just to ensure that the chocolate crumble sticks to the balls. So, instead, cover the palms of your gloves in melted chocolate and roll the balls between your hands. This will ensure that they're not dripping with melted chocolate, and only have a thin coating. The other team member just needs to shake the bowl with the chocolate crumble around to cover the balls. Once covered, you're done.

If you want Bruce's Balls to be dense and fudgy, keep them in the fridge. If you'd prefer them to be cakey and a bit less rich, keep them at room temperature. Why not keep one in the fridge and one on the kitchen side? Multi-textural ball party – count me in. They'll keep perfectly well for 5 days. You can freeze them for up to a month, but the crumble might lose some of its crunch.

BRUCE'S JUICES

The ultimate bonus track. Just when you thought it was over, I throw a Bruce milkshake in your face. Not literally, you're not that special. It's only right that the only beverage in this book revolves around Bruce. Then again, can you really call something a beverage if it's packed full of chocolate cake? Drink up.

INGREDIENTS

80g (2¾oz) double (heavy) cream
100g (3½oz) Bruce cake sponge
100g (3½oz) chocolate ice cream
50g (1¾oz) 55% dark chocolate, melted
50g (1¾oz) whole milk
5g (⅛oz) sea salt
30g (1oz) expen$ive sprinkles, to serve

METHOD

Start by whipping the cream, following the method for Properly Whipped Cream on page 84. Once whipped, spoon into a piping (pastry) bag, and refrigerate.

Put the cake, ice cream, melted chocolate, milk, and sea salt in a blender and blend on high speed until thick and creamy. If preferred, you can blend everything except the cake, and mix this in by hand afterwards, resulting in bigger pieces of sponge, making it more of an eat with a spoon kind of affair.

Pour the milkshake into your favourite glass and top with the whipped cream. Finish with sprinkles and drink through the most over-the-top straw that you can find.

INDEX

THANKS

I'd like to begin by thanking my mum. I wouldn't be here without her. Not only do I mean that literally, because she birthed me, but because in the early days of GET BAKED®, she let me operate the business from her kitchen. I don't tell her enough how much I love her, but I think this will make up for it, because it's now in writing.

Thank you to my sister Marnie, who I'm incredibly close to, and my brother-in-law Phil, for the support and belief they've shown me from day one, even when things weren't going according to plan.

My darling wife Amy, who deserves a medal for putting up with me. You have been with me at my worst, and occasionally seen me at my best. Without you, I wouldn't be able to function, let alone write this book.

To my daughter Sage, who isn't old enough to be able to read this yet, I love you more than you could ever imagine, and hopefully I make you as proud of me, as I am of you.

Lakey, who has been with the business since day one. It's been quite the journey. You understand this brand better than anyone, and I know how much the business means to you. I am so grateful for your continued commitment to GET BAKED®.

Laura, who runs our bakery, and keeps me in business. Your hard work is incredibly appreciated, and thank you for making almost all of the stuff photographed in this book. Seeing as I've forgotten how to bake. Just kidding. Kinda.

Thank you to Kate for building the magnificent Bruce that was used in this book. I'm delighted for you that you now have a famous thumb.

To Ellis, who produced all of the amazing photography inside this book, Vic for her prop styling magic, Bella for all her editing and my publisher Jess for giving me the opportunity to share these recipes with the world.

Our success is owed almost entirely to the team working at our store in Headingley, and our production bakery in Leeds. I am very lucky to have people working with the business that genuinely care, and do their best day in, day out.

I must also thank our customers. We are so unbelievably lucky to have such a loyal following, and so many of them have been with us through the good times, and the bad. I am incredibly grateful to all of you.

Lastly, I'd like to thank my dad. I wish more than anything that he was here to read this book. My passion for food, and the drive to do something meaningful with that passion, is all because of him.

Q The Quarto Group

Brimming with creative inspiration, how-to projects, and useful information to enrich your everyday life, quarto.com is a favourite destination for those pursuing their interests and passions.

First published in 2023 by White Lion Publishing, an imprint of The Quarto Group
One Triptych Place, London, SE1 9SH, United Kingdom
www.Quarto.com

ISBN 978-0-7112-7971-1
Ebook ISBN 978-0-7112-7972-8

10 9 8 7 6 5 4 3 2 1

Photographer & Art Director: Ellis Parrinder
Prop stylist: Victoria Twyman
Publisher: Jessica Axe
Editorial Director: Nicky Hill
Editor: Bella Skertchly
Copy-editor: Laura Nickoll
Design: Evi-O.Studio | Wilson Leung, Katherine Zhang, Kait Polkinghorne & Susan Le

Printed in China